fearless
prayer

Craig Hazen

HARVEST HOUSE PUBLISHERS
EUGENE, OREGON

Cover by Aesthetic Soup

Fearless Prayer
Copyright © 2018 Craig Hazen
Published by Harvest House Publishers
Eugene, Oregon 97408
www.harvesthousepublishers.com

ISBN 978-0-7369-7379-3 (pbk.)
ISBN 978-0-7369-7380-9 (eBook)

Library of Congress Cataloging-in-Publication Data is on file at the Library of Congress, Washington, DC.

Printed in the United States of America

20 21 22 23 24 25 26 / VP-SK / 10 9 8 7 6 5 4 3

CONTENTS

†

CHAPTER 1

Awakening to the Words of Jesus

Over a decade ago I was sitting in my comfy Bible-reading chair immersed in the Gospel of John. I have a large family and I get up earlier than everyone else, so I normally get a bit of solitude in the morning to read the Bible and pray. This particular morning I was in chapter 15 reading something I must have read a few dozen times before. For some reason, this time one of the verses came alive to me, but not in the typical way people report having a Bible verse speak to them. Oh, it spoke to me all right. But the message that came to me was: "You don't really believe this."

The verse in question was John 15:7. It is a challenging statement that Jesus uttered in the middle of a talk to his disciples often called the vine and the branches discourse. The verse says this: "If you remain in me and my words remain in you, ask whatever you wish, and it will be done for you."

I think the monologue in my mind that morning was not very profound. It went something like,

> *Huh, I wonder what that's all about?*
> *That doesn't seem to be a real thing.*
> *I don't treat it like it's real.*
> *And I don't think I know anybody*
> *who treats it like it's real.*
> *If some do treat it like it's real, they're probably*
> *part of that "name it and claim it" movement.*
> *Maybe this is meant for the apostles themselves*
> *or spiritual superstars like Billy Graham.*
> *I'll bet you that people who do take it too*
> *seriously are a little spiritually weird.*
> *Hmm, it says we have to "remain."*
> *We're probably not doing that, whatever that is.*

Looking back on it, this important verse was, in my mind, dying the death of a thousand qualifications. I simply wasn't going to take it seriously at that point—even though these were words spoken by Jesus himself and recorded in the Bible that I deeply believe is the Word of God. My functional approach was, "Hey, there is plenty in the Bible that makes more sense than this. So I'll just stick with that stuff. Movin' on!"

Well, the Holy Spirit had some different plans for me. He kept the issue about the true meaning of this verse alive in me to the point where I had to investigate it. And I couldn't be more grateful for his intervention. I really had no idea how committed God is to answering our prayers and how thrilled he is when we ask. Studying this verse, and many more like it, has been a tremendously rewarding and enlightening time for me. And I am eager to share some of my findings with you.

TO REKINDLE A SUPERNATURAL MINDSET

My hope for this book is that it might help to rekindle a supernatural mindset in believers of every stripe so that we can put this amazing promise to work in our lives for the kingdom's sake. Here is a truism: Life is difficult. Here is another truism: Life is doubly difficult when we seek to do important kingdom work. We need this promise to be fulfilled or we will be spinning our wheels far more than we should be. In verse 5 of the same passage, Jesus said, "Apart from me you can do nothing." Of course *that* we *can* believe.

But I want to see if we can't come to terms with the flip side of verse 5, that is, with him we can do anything—which is a solid biblical teaching.

So, let's take the plunge and find out what the rest of God's Word, thoughtful scholars, and solid spiritual understanding say about the true meaning of John 15:7. Let's see if we can't sort out what gives us such deep hesitation in embracing this amazing promise. Let's see if we can't set aside the ideas, interpretations, and behaviors that keep us from fearless prayer and realizing the Lord's astonishing promise to us.

CHAPTER 2

Does This Stuff Really Happen?

I had the rare opportunity to study some of the great world religious traditions in some depth when I did a PhD in religious studies at the University of California. Comparing my Christianity to the other major religions was an eye-opening experience. Some features of Christianity set it apart in rather dramatic fashion from other faiths.

One feature that made Christianity unique was the sheer volume of legitimate, documentable testimonies and traditions of answered prayer. In fact, I'm sure that if you are a follower of Jesus Christ, you can add to the unending collection of firsthand accounts.

I start off with four examples of answered prayer that all have something very important in common. As you read them, I don't know that you will see the common thread immediately—good job if you do. But what these accounts have in common has the potential to revolutionize not just your prayer life, but also your ministry and your relationship with God as well.

The Lord himself encourages us to offer up fearless prayers. We worship and pray to a God who loves us very much and longs for us to bear wonderful spiritual fruit through him. In order to do that, he has promised to meet us and to provide for us in remarkable ways. And he has promised that if we abide in him and his words abide in us, that we can ask for anything and we shall have it.

CRYPTIC CONNECTION

I was finished giving my guest lectures at a university in the Midwest. They really kept me busy morning, noon, and night with speaking, meetings, and meals. I gave my final talk at noon and then headed for a small airport. I needed everything on the trip home to go well because I had a lecture scheduled for that night in Southern California, and then very important ministry meetings the next morning. A serious delay would really wreak havoc.

My first flight was to Atlanta on a small commuter jet. I

was going to connect in Atlanta and then on to Los Angeles. It was going to be a long day of travel. But it looked like it was going to be even longer because my first flight was late. We weren't going to board until over an hour beyond our scheduled departure time, which could cause me to miss my second, longer flight. (None of this is news to those of you who travel frequently.)

So we finally boarded the small jet. It was full and the seats were small and it was going to be a couple of hours of less-than-comfortable travel. I distinctly remember settling into my seat and praying that I would make the connection. Sometimes in prayer I make my case with God—as if he needs to hear my reasoning on the matter. But hey, that's what some of the key players in the Bible did too, so I'm in good company. I never pray with a lot of words, so my entire petition was something like, "God I really think you were instrumental in setting up what is happening in LA tonight and tomorrow. And I think it has potential to bear fruit for the kingdom. Hear this humble request: Get me there on time. Oh, and I also pray for a more comfortable seat for the next flight. Amen." I don't hesitate to throw in those extras because I know God loves me and likes to give me encouraging gifts once in a while.

My hope was that the small plane would make up some

time in the air so that I could make my connection. But as we approached a rainy Atlanta, I was constantly looking at my watch. It was going to be so close. The moment I could, I opened the airline app on my phone and discovered my next gate was way across the airport. It would take me fifteen minutes just to get from gate to gate. I was almost certainly not going to make it. Long-shot alternative plans were already starting to race through my mind.

When I got to the exit door of the plane, a woman wearing a dark suit was standing just outside the door. She had an electronic sign in her hand that said HAZEN on it. I said to her, "I'm Craig Hazen," and she immediately grabbed the suitcase out of my hand and said only, "Follow me." She then walked through a forbidden door right out of the boarding ramp. I hesitated for a moment because I didn't have a badge or a code or whatever is necessary to walk out onto an active tarmac at the busiest airport in the world.

Another woman in a dark suit met me on the platform just outside the door and opened an umbrella to hold over me as she escorted me down the stairs following the woman with my suitcase. I had no idea who they were. FBI? Secret Service? Very serious librarians looking for a book I hadn't returned? What? At the bottom of the stairs was a beautiful black Porsche Cayenne SUV. The woman with my suitcase opened the back hatch and put my suitcase in. The other woman opened the door to the backseat for me, and I got in and buckled up. Both of them got in the front seats. Strangely I remember thinking that was a positive sign because they didn't feel the need to guard me in the backseat. The driver then tore out onto active airline taxiways heading across the airport. We even got a little air on one of the whoop-dee-doos as we raced through highly restricted areas.

They finally pulled up alongside some stairs connected to the boarding ramp of a Boeing 757 parked at a gate. They leaped out of the SUV onto the tarmac. One grabbed my suitcase and the other opened an umbrella to cover me as they led me up the stairs. They walked me right through the outside door of the boarding ramp and into the 757. Once in, they turned left at the aisle right into the first-class cabin, put my suitcase in an awaiting space in the overhead bin, pointed to an aisle seat—the only seat left in first class, and maybe the only one left on the airplane. They then rushed off the plane, exiting just seconds before the aircraft doors were closed and secured.

Then I heard the first words since the initial "Follow me." "Mr. Hazen, can I get you anything to drink before we depart?"

What just happened?

VAN TO HAND WARMTH

It can turn cold at night in Phoenix in the winter, and sometimes the homeless people are caught unprepared—no warm clothes, no warm blankets. James Taylor was a pastor at a small church in Phoenix that organized a simple service project to deliver blankets to people living on the street. They were able to purchase thirty-five new blankets to distribute. They prayed for blessing on their work and that the people who needed the blankets most would receive them. Pastor James was going to make the delivery.

James knew just where to go to find those in need and drove up to find a dozen or so people warming themselves by a trash-can fire. He offered them blankets right out of the window of his van. The first couple of new blanket owners seemed surprised and very grateful. James reached for another armful of blankets as several more hands quickly appeared through his open window. James was now handing out blankets as fast as he could grab them, and he was glad he had locked all the doors.

But then panic struck Pastor James. Not because he was afraid of the mob, but because he was afraid he did not have enough blankets for everyone who wanted one.

A small woman squeezed her way through to James's

window, but she wasn't reaching out to grab a blanket. Her arms were wrapped tightly around her torso trying to keep herself warm with only the paper-thin jacket she had on. James gave her a blanket, but it was the last one. Standing behind the woman was a tall man with a scraggly beard and desperation in his eyes. He asked, "May I have a blanket too?" James was brokenhearted to tell the man, "Brother, that was the last new blanket. But wait…" James thought he had a couple of older blankets, used and worn, hiding behind the seat. He looked back to see if he could grab one and saw two new blankets in their packaging.

James remembers, "As I picked them up, it dawned on me that those new ones hadn't been there before. I'd given them all out—I was sure of it." Another couple of hands appeared at his window, and again he turned to rummage for an old blanket, only to discover two more new ones. This happened several more times. He finally put a new blanket into the very last hand at his window.

"I started with thirty-five blankets and I gave out at least fifty," James said. As he pulled his van away from the scene, he heard people say, "God bless you, mister." And in awe at the love and power of God, he replied, "He already did!"[1]

PRAYER LANGUAGE

In 1888 a courageous missionary couple, Rosalind and Jonathan Goforth, was appointed by the Canadian Presbyterian Church to open a new mission field in Henan Province, China. It was known at the time to be the part of China with the most intolerance toward foreigners.

Most of the Goforths' language learning was going to take place in the country. It was a huge challenge to learn a difficult language well enough to get by day to day. It was an even bigger challenge to learn it well enough to be an effective evangelist. Even though Jonathan Goforth gave the language his full attention for many hours every day, according to his wife's account, the language acquisition was going painfully slow.

Jonathan and a missionary colleague regularly went to a street chapel they had set up to practice preaching in Chinese to the people. Rosalind wrote, "But though Mr. Goforth had come to China almost a year before the other missionary, the people would ask the latter to speak instead of Mr. Goforth, saying they understood him better." It was a monumental struggle, and Jonathan seemed to be losing.

Not long after this, he admitted to his wife that he might not be cut out for this. "If the Lord does not give me some very special help in this language, I fear I shall be a failure as a missionary."

Only hours later Jonathan returned home from the chapel with sheer delight on his face. When his time had come to speak, words and phrases flowed like never before. Not only had he made himself understood, but many also appeared deeply moved by what he had to say. Some even came up to him afterward to talk about his message. This sudden and unexpected upturn in his language abilities was something he featured prominently in his diary entry for that day.

About two and a half months later, Jonathan received a letter from a student at Knox College, a Presbyterian school in Illinois. The letter focused on a prayer meeting some students had recently attended. At this meeting the students specifically prayed for the Goforths, and while they were praying, they felt God's presence in unique and palpable ways, and their prayers seemed especially powerful. It had such an impact on the students that one of them decided to write Jonathan to see if he had noticed any special move of God in his life at that time. When Jonathan consulted his diary and compared it with the students' time of prayer, it was an exact match. The quantum leap in language ability had been God's response to some faithful prayer supporters on the home front.[2]

JAIL BREAK

An ancient historian named Luke recorded the following remarkable event.

> It was about this time that King Herod arrested some who belonged to the church, intending to persecute them. He had James, the brother of John, put to death with the sword. When he saw that this met with approval among the Jews, he proceeded to seize Peter also. This happened during the Festival of Unleavened Bread. After arresting him, he put him in prison, handing him over to be guarded by four squads of four soldiers each. Herod intended to bring him out for public trial after the Passover.
>
> So Peter was kept in prison, but the church was earnestly praying to God for him.
>
> The night before Herod was to bring him to trial, Peter was sleeping between two soldiers, bound with two chains, and sentries stood guard at the entrance. Suddenly an angel of the Lord appeared and a light shone in the cell. He struck Peter on the side and woke him up. "Quick, get up!" he said, and the chains fell off Peter's wrists.

Then the angel said to him, "Put on your clothes and sandals." And Peter did so. "Wrap your cloak around you and follow me," the angel told him. Peter followed him out of the prison, but he had no idea that what the angel was doing was really happening; he thought he was seeing a vision. They passed the first and second guards and came to the iron gate leading to the city. It opened for them by itself, and they went through it. When they had walked the length of one street, suddenly the angel left him.

Then Peter came to himself and said, "Now I know without a doubt that the Lord has sent his angel and rescued me from Herod's clutches and from everything the Jewish people were hoping would happen."

When this had dawned on him, he went to the house of Mary the mother of John, also called Mark, where many people had gathered and were praying (Acts 12:1-12).

CHAPTER 3

Prayer: Strange, Powerful, and Real

Years ago I was asked to be the guest host for a popular radio talk program. The regular host was out of town, and the producers didn't want to play a repeat show from the archives. So I was the replacement.

It was going to be a live weekend broadcast, but when I arrived at the radio station, the parking lot was empty. I went into an office tower, up an elevator, and rang a bell at the door of an office suite owned by the station. After a long wait, someone came to let me in. It was the producer for the show. We walked into a good-sized facility that was eerily silent and dim because there wasn't a soul there apart from the two of us. It was a sea of cubicles with a cluster of specialized, soundproof broadcast booths in the back. Almost no lights were on except for some dim lights coming from the booths.

We walked into the booth I would be using and sat down. It was about the size of an office cubicle but completely enclosed and decked out with broadcasting gear. The producer walked me through a few of the details about how to field calls, how best to get into and out of commercial breaks, and generally how we were going to silently signal each other through the window.

"We'll be on in three minutes," he said as he handed me the headphones, adjusted the microphone in front of me, closed the door to my booth, and walked to the one next to it.

"Two minutes," he said in a very short burst I could hear in my headphones.

I'm not a naturally talkative guy (which is exactly why I don't have my own radio program), so I over-prepare. I know several guys who do radio, and all of them seem to be able to talk easier than they can breathe. They are truly wired for the job. But I had a good stack of paper in front of me with all kinds of topics ready in case callers were few and far between. I didn't want dead air—next to cursing a blue streak, the worst thing you can have in radio.

"One minute."

So there I sat, opening comments on paper in front of me ready to go. I had done radio before, but it was in a bustling weekday environment with lots of action surrounding the broadcast booth—so much action that for an occasional guest host like me, it was a challenge to stay focused. This time with empty offices, it felt like broadcasting from a graveyard.

"Thirty seconds."

It was too small to be a panic attack, so I'll call it a "dread spasm." Everything was on track. The equipment was ready to hum, and I was busy having a last sip of water when a strange mixture of doubt and fear with a dash of claustrophobia gripped me. It wasn't doubt about my ability to do the job. It was far more irrational than that. *Who is going to hear me? Who is out there listening?* It might be how one of the early solo astronauts like Alan Shepard, John Glenn, or Major Tom felt sitting in a "tin can far above the world." I was sitting in a small, dimly lit space and the windows were simply returning a reflection of me and the contents of the booth. The producer was next door, but not in view.

The on-air light came to life at the same time the dread spasm landed in my breastbone. I think I would have been fine had a human being been sitting across the desk nodding, smiling, and ready to interact with me. But all I saw was my reflection in the window and the microphone in front of me. I was either going to be talking to myself or trusting that the microphone was going to carry my voice to thousands of people.

Fortunately, I didn't go down in flames. The producer simply played the intro music just a moment or two longer than normal. I finally gulped some air and began my opening comments.

PRAYER AS A VIGOROUS DEMONSTRATION OF FAITH

Prayer might be the preeminent exercise of faith. From a worldly standpoint it is a very strange practice. Think about it. You try to carve out some precious time and find a quiet spot where you can have a bit of solitude. Then you sit there by yourself and begin talking—either saying the words in your mind or with your mouth—without a single indicator in the physical realm that what you are doing has any grounding in reality.

My experience in the radio booth had a similar texture. There was a decent amount of faith involved. I spoke into the microphone, and I had to trust that my voice was being converted into radio waves that were beamed out for miles

in every direction. Then I had to trust that there were people with radio receivers on the other end who could hear
my voice as it was recreated from the waves. It wasn't until
the calls started coming in from real people responding to
my comments that my irrational "dread spasm" finally fully
dissipated.

The strange experience of radio broadcasting actually
has a lot more immediate confirmation going for it than
prayer does—at least in a radio booth there are lights flash-
ing and needles bouncing. And then you finally get to hear
the voices coming back at you. Not so with prayer—at least
not in the same way.

So even if you are someone who prays infrequently and
simply, perhaps you are new to it all, you are still engag-
ing in a solid step of faith. You are showing that you trust
enough to engage in this strange Christian ritual of speaking out words to an unseen world with some degree of hope
that God is there, that he can hear you, and that he might
just respond in word or deed. And this small step of faith can
go a long way. Perhaps this is what Jesus had in mind when
he said, "Truly I tell you, if you have faith as small as a mus-
tard seed, you can say to this mountain, 'Move from here to
there,' and it will move. Nothing will be impossible for you"
(Matthew 17:20). Talk about encouraging a newbie!

THE NATURE OF PRAYER

There are shelves and shelves of books devoted to the subject of prayer. One common feature of these books is that, no matter how experienced the authors are or how much they have researched the matter, they admit up front that they *struggle* with this crucial Christian activity. Even a spiritual luminary and scholar like J.I. Packer wrote that "we are all…poor strugglers in our experience of praying."[1] So if you're new to prayer, or have crashed and burned many times over in your attempts at meaningful prayer, be of good cheer. You certainly are not alone. And just in case you think that because I am writing an upbeat book on prayer that I don't struggle, that would not be true. I struggle along with the rest. It just comes with the territory. The occasional struggle, though, is well worth it.

On its surface, prayer is not complex or confusing. Prayer is conversation or communication with God. Most of us possess basic communication skills already. So presumably if we can converse with other humans successfully, we have the essential tool set we need to communicate with God.

Now I don't want to make it sound as though it's exactly like chatting with your neighbor over the backyard fence. Clearly there are some key differences in play when one is conversing with an invisible being who can speak billions of galaxies into existence! Not only might we be intimidated by his immense power, knowledge, and holiness, but we also might be overwhelmed to consider the kinds of resources he brings to the table. Yet he invites us. He is a loving Creator and Father who has made it abundantly clear that he wants to hear from us, to interact with us, to have a full-fledged family relationship that involves close conversation.

PRAYER AS ASKING

It is a part of our culture in the USA to be reluctant to ask people for things. If you have traveled to Canada or Britain, you have probably noticed that the reluctance is even greater there. Now, we all do ask for things from others, but generally our culture is not comfortable with the practice— especially asking for help or favors. Social scientists have come up with a range of possible reasons for this: general shyness, fear of rejection, vulnerability, a fragile ego, being a burden, carrying a strong sense of independence, and more.

I feel this reluctance myself. I sense that in me it stems from a desire not to impose upon another person. I figure they are already busy and burdened enough without having to add my request to the list. I often use a phrase (I learned it from a

Canadian) that demonstrates my lack of comfort with asking someone for help or a favor. I regularly say, "Can I trouble you to [*insert whatever the request might be*]?" For example, "Can I trouble you to pass the milk?" "Can I trouble you to repeat your email address?" My common way of asking reveals in a stark way my reluctance to burden someone to exert themselves on my behalf. Many of us carry this around with us and don't think much about it. And this is a great irony for devout Christians in our culture because prayer is essentially *asking*.

Prayer is asking. We can qualify this statement if we need to by saying prayer is asking in relationship, prayer is asking in conversation, prayer is asking with the goal of making us mature in Christ, prayer is asking while being conformed to God's will, and so on. But in essence, after all the add-ons are factored in, prayer is asking.

In his book on prayer, Packer wrote, "But at the core, where all people of prayer bend their knees, prayer is asking, begging God to supply felt needs. In a broad sense, asking is the very essence of praying…All books on prayer affirm this, all who ever pray feel this, and all religions whatever their view of God or gods, agree on this."[2] Dallas Willard concurred: "The picture of prayer that emerges from the life and teachings of Jesus in the Gospels is quite clear. Basically, it is one of asking, requesting things from God."[3]

Surely the most authoritative word on prayer comes from Jesus himself when he takes on the challenge offered up by one of his disciples to "teach us to pray" (Luke 11:1). Jesus then teaches them what we know as the Lord's Prayer (Luke 11:2-4 and Matthew 6:9-13). And as knowledgeable commentators have pointed out through the centuries, the Lord's Prayer is a set of six requests, six "asks" directed to "Our Father in heaven." Prayer is fundamentally asking. Since this is true based on the authority of Jesus himself, and since prayer is so central to a dynamic life with God, it makes sense for us to learn how to ask—to ask regularly, fearlessly, sincerely, expectantly, and humbly for his hand to move in our lives in all the right ways.

WHY WE DON'T ASK,
AND WHY WE SHOULD

Our cultural reluctance to ask for things is certainly a hurdle for our spiritual life. So we need to spend a little time thinking about how we can carve out a different path than the one our culture encourages when approaching God with requests.

First, we need to remember to whom we are directing our requests. God, our heavenly Father, is eternal, all-knowing, all-powerful, everywhere present, and perfectly good. He willed into existence everything in the cosmos from angels to souls, from quarks to quasars. He is not a single mom working her second job of the day, dead tired and with barely two nickels to rub together. Anyone would be smart to hesitate to make a burdensome request of the harried single parent barely making it, but God does not run out of energy or resources for his children.

Second, God is love. He loves us and will always, always want what's best for us. He wants us to run from sin and run to him. Even more so than the most loving gracious human fathers, God delights in giving us what we request. As Jesus said in Matthew 7:11, "If you, then, though you are evil, know how to give good gifts to your children, how much more will your Father in heaven give good gifts to those who ask him!"

Third, asking God through prayer to help us requires our having a relationship with God—something God delights in and for which he rewards us. "But when you pray, go into your room, close the door and pray to your Father, who is unseen. Then your Father, who sees what is done in secret, will reward you" (Matthew 6:6). Clearly we can go much further in our relationship with God through prayer than simply making requests. But it is a powerful place to start and a feature of prayer that will always be with us no matter how spiritually mature we get. And besides, God set it up that way. Even in his final hours before the cross, Jesus himself was making weighty requests of the Father flowing through their profound love relationship.

Fourth, being in a relationship in which asking is a central and desirable element makes dependence on God a daily feature, if not a moment by moment feature. The Lord wants us to be people of increasing faith—consulting him and trusting him for everything as we "pray continually" (1 Thessalonians 5:17). Because of his goal for us, he welcomes our requests. And it can snowball. As we trust him enough to lay our requests before him, he answers. The answers we see then build our faith to where we ask him for much weightier things.

> In the morning, LORD, you hear my voice;
>   in the morning I lay my requests before you
>   and wait expectantly (Psalm 5:3).

"Very truly I tell you, whoever believes in me will do the works I have been doing, and they will do even greater things than these, because I am going to the Father. And I will do whatever you ask in my name, so that the Father may be glorified in the Son" (John 14:12-13).

In the Lord's Prayer, Jesus taught us to ask, "Give us *today* our daily bread" (Matthew 6:11). Jesus really wants us to focus in on the *daily* nature of his provision. *Today, each day*, we are to ask in prayer for our meals. Unless we are fasting, we will need food today. Our daily need for food should drive us to the Father every day. And God would have it no other way.

He is near to us, he wants us to ask, and we depend on his provision day by day. In a country where supermarkets overflow with food, this might not seem a matter of immediate dependence for us. But in some parts of the world right now, "Give us today our daily bread" are life-sustaining words. And they may be life-sustaining words for us in a day yet to come.

Our daily need and our daily asking highlight our dependence on God. This is just where he wants us.

Fifth, God likes our requests so much that he invites us to make them again and again—even to the point of (our) annoyance. Persistence in asking is an unmistakable feature of Jesus's teaching on prayer. We are not talking about incessant repetition of magical phrases, and not the kind of "pagan babbling" rejected by Jesus in Matthew 6:7-8. No, we are talking about bringing God our requests day by day until they are resolved. He wants us to keep our most important prayer issues on the front burner. He wants us to know that he cares about them and that we trust he will address them in his perfect timing.

Jesus uses two parables to illustrate this feature of Christian prayer. The first one in Luke 18 is traditionally called the "Parable of the Persistent Widow." Luke opens the passage with a clear purpose statement: "Then Jesus told his disciples a parable to show them that they should always pray and never give up" (18:1). He then records Jesus's story about a widow who wanted to get justice against her adversary in front of a judge who kept refusing her many requests. Finally, after many visits, the judge, who held all the cards and who didn't fear God or people, relented. He said, "because this widow keeps bothering me, I will see that she gets justice, so that she won't eventually come and attack me!" (18:5). The lesson is that if this corrupt judge will see that justice is done because of the persistence of the widow, *how much more* will *God* hear us and take action.

On another occasion Jesus taught a parable with a similar message. Just after teaching the Lord's Prayer to the disciples in Luke 11, Jesus adds a parable to emphasize the need for persistence. Suppose you go to a friend at midnight and ask for three loaves of bread to feed a traveler who suddenly appeared at your door very late. Your friend says, "Don't bother me. The kids are in bed and the door is locked for the night." Jesus concludes the story with this: "I tell you, even though he will not get up and give you the bread because of friendship, yet because of your shameless audacity he will surely get up and give you as much as you need" (Luke 11:8).

Again the argument is this: If a reluctant, annoyed neighbor will give you what you ask for due to your persistence, *how much more* will your loving heavenly Father give to you what you ask. To emphasize persistence in prayer over and above this parable, Jesus follows up with this: "So I say to you: Ask and it will be given to you; seek and you will find; knock and the door will be opened to you. For everyone who asks receives; the one who seeks finds; and to the one who knocks, the door will be opened" (11:9-10). In a strange turnabout, Jesus is persistently asking us to be persistent in asking. Anything that Jesus emphasized to this degree, we need to embed deeply within our souls. We are to be persistent in asking through prayer.

Sixth, asking daily is a gateway to other important spiritual disciplines that not only enhance our Christian life, but also circle back and enhance our life of prayer, our personal communion with God. Regular prayer is inevitably accompanied by other spiritual practices that are vital to maturity in Christ. Some of these are the study of God's Word, Christian meditation, worship, thanksgiving, confession of sin, solitude, and fasting. Daily petitionary prayer is the start. But once these all come together, it will turn a low-voltage spiritual life into something beyond measure—a way of "co-laboring with God to accomplish good things and advance his Kingdom purposes."[4]

Including worship, thanksgiving, and confession of sin into times of prayer is a wonderful thing to do—and should be done. I've noticed, though, that some lessons and studies on prayer emphasize these to the exclusion or dilution of asking—as if asking is a less than worthy aspect of prayer. They seem to see asking as more self-centered or not truly spiritual. According to James, asking certainly can go awry, and we need to guard against that (see James 4:3). But once our safeguards are in place, we need to ask. We need to ask regularly, boldly, and with expectation. And we need to remember that asking, or petitionary prayer, is not a lesser form of prayer. Rather it is what the Lord himself taught us to do.

SURE FOOTING AS WE MOVE FORWARD

A chapter on prayer can seem rather mystical, ethereal, or otherworldly—especially if you are new to the practice or unfamiliar with it. Clearly there are a lot of assumptions being made about God, Jesus, the Bible, the invisible world, and the truth of Christianity. If you are like me, you want to know that all of this talk about prayer is grounded in something solid. You want to know that it is grounded in something other than a few people's inner spiritual experience.

One thing I have found enormously helpful over the years in grounding my prayer life and my spiritual communion with God is understanding that at the heart of the Christian faith sits a treasure trove of reason, evidence, facts, and clear thinking that demonstrate that Christianity is true beyond a shadow of a doubt.

Before moving on to our primary text in the Gospel of John, it won't hurt one bit to review the generous trail of evidence that God left us that traces back to the Lord Jesus Christ—his sinless life, his miracles, his teachings on prayer, his death on a cross, and his resurrection from the dead. This is all real, and God wants us to know that it's real. This will give sure footing as we move into the later chapters and discover an amazing promise of God.

CHAPTER 4

Reasons to Believe

Testimonies from committed followers of Jesus about answered prayers are numerous and profound. Sometimes these answers come in dramatic fashion, and sometimes they arrive in ways that are so seamless with the course of life that it takes a while to notice them. To be sure, occasionally I don't notice answered prayer until I look at my prayer journal and am reminded of what exactly I've been praying for.

Hearing such testimonies about God's faithfulness to his people's petitions, and reading books and articles about them, can't help but bolster our trust in God and his Word about prayer. However, as helpful as these testimonies are in boosting our trust, they are merely scratches on the surface. God delights in much more than showing his fatherly

37

devotion and kindness to us through answered prayer. He loves to put his glory on display so that anyone who seeks the truth about him and his Word simply can't ignore the profound evidence and sound reasoning that provides us sure knowledge of God and his free gift of salvation. Knowing how God delights in demonstrating the general truth of his identity and his Word certainly is helpful in trusting that he exists and that he is able to hear our prayers and to act on them.

A SATISFIED HEART AND MIND

The evidence and the clear reasoning that God provides in order to confirm the gospel are especially near and dear to my heart. Reason and evidence were powerful tools God used to win me over.

I became a Christian as a senior in high school. Before that I probably could have been considered the village atheist or agnostic on my campus. My thinking at the time was that God probably did not exist and that religions, including Christianity, were based almost entirely on myth, legend, and personal feelings. But I also had a strong backup position: Even if I were wrong and God did exist and some religion or religions were true, there would be no way to *know* these things to be true. In my view at the time, religions were inherently unknowable. Lack of knowledge was actually a key defining feature of religion.

I was quite certain that my backup position was right because the religious people I encountered never had any evidence or facts to present to me. How could they have knowledge without facts, evidence, or reason? They simply told me that it was all about faith. And the way they described their faith was really no different than blind leaping, where you make a deep commitment to something for which you have no good reason to believe that it's true. Or, even worse, you commit to some belief even though you have reasons to suspect the belief is false. There was no way that I was going to do that.

In high school I was captivated by the sciences and had that special mental wiring to excel in them. In college I majored in biology and ran a research lab. In my mind, the sciences were all about evidence, reason, and proof leading to *real* knowledge. Christianity seemed to be the exact opposite. All religions, in fact, seemed to offer only blind leaping along with a very slim hope that one might feel better about life, death, and the painful mysteries of the cosmos, at least for a time. Comparing science with religion seemed to me like a standoff between solid reason and blind faith. And the choice between those two was obvious to a scientifically minded person.

Then everything changed.

A high-school friend invited me to go with her to a vibrant, Bible-centered church. I was curious and thought, *What harm could it do?* So I went. Well, I heard a magnificent presentation of the gospel and was so deeply moved by it all that I went forward during an altar call. (Wow, was the friend who brought me shocked. It turned out a number of Christians at my high school were praying for me, the hard-boiled campus skeptic.) Looking back now, of course, I was being moved by the Holy Spirit to take the plunge—and did so joyfully with an attitude of spiritual experimentation.

I felt something deep inside at the time, as though the process of inner change was already underway. During that special moment in the church, I was beginning the move from darkness to light. The gospel seed had been planted and it was already starting to germinate.

However, something else took place in the days and weeks after that event that was equally important. You see, I was still asking the same troublesome questions I had been asking before my apparent divine encounter. But this time it was different. This time when I asked my questions, mature Christians were doing their best to answer them—and doing a pretty fair job of it. And God bless them, if they did not have an answer to something, they put excellent books into my hands, told me about informative radio programs I might listen to, and loaded me up with cassette tapes (yes, it was that long ago) of lectures from some of the smartest, best-credentialed scholars I had ever heard. These brilliant Christians gave clear, in-depth, and penetrating answers to the toughest questions about the Christian faith. They were actually inviting skeptics like me to bring it on. These scholars did not consider Christianity something into which one needed to leap blindly. Rather, they considered the Scriptures to be true in all they taught and that Christianity was a religion that invited people to enter in with their eyes wide open, asking hard questions all the way. Christianity could handle it—because Christianity was true.

Although I had *felt* something profound when I heard the gospel—and I look back fondly on that moment as a special gift from God—what came next was equally profound. Having clear answers to my sincere questions about the Christian faith was powerful. During the days and weeks following my church experience, God forged a tight bond between my heart and my mind as satisfying answers flooded in to objectively confirm the authenticity of all the feelings I couldn't fully explain.

Hearing solid answers so early on in my spiritual life, and coming to know that the Christian tradition was devoted to providing such answers, had a multiplier effect on my staying power with the Lord. I never turned back. Based on the evidence, there was simply no other game in town. I felt like Peter in John 6:68 where he said to Jesus, "Lord, to whom shall we go? You have the words of eternal life."

And then, because I knew personally how important answers like these were to persuading skeptics and unbelievers, I became devoted to providing answers myself. I ended up doing a PhD in religious studies where I was able to compare the claims, the evidence, and the reasoning at the core of all the world's great religions. I founded a graduate program in Christian apologetics at Biola University that became one of the largest and most prestigious programs of its kind on the planet. And after forty-plus years of searching out and offering answers, I still wake up about every other morning amazed in a fresh way at the true intellectual feast Christianity serves up.

No one has to check his intellect at the door before entering the church that Jesus founded. Not only is Christianity true, but it also brings coherence, color, and life to everything else we experience in our world. As C.S Lewis wrote, "I believe in Christianity as I believe that the sun has risen:

not only because I see it, but because by it I see everything else." So we can claim to *know* that Christianity is true, and not just through some inner spiritual knowledge. Rather, we can know it to be true objectively—that is, outside of our inner experience—through a careful examination of the facts of history, science, philosophy, or any other area of human inquiry we can bring to the table. Christianity is the true story of all that ever was, is, or will be. And by his grace, God left us a generous trail of evidence testifying inwardly and outwardly to all that he did or said on our behalf, so that we can have truly satisfied hearts *and minds*.

DEBILITATING DOUBT

I hope the connection between prayer and the overall truth of Christianity is an obvious one to you. Many things hinder the believer's prayer life, such as sin, poor relationships, guilt, unforgiveness, and worldliness. But there is another hindrance that can march shoulder to shoulder with any in this list in derailing vibrant communication with God, and that is *doubt*.

If a Christian is struggling with the existence of God, the reality of the afterlife, Jesus as fully God and fully man, the historicity of the resurrection, or the trustworthiness of the Bible, then it makes perfect sense that he will be far less likely to pray or have confidence that God will respond. Deep doubt has the potential to wreak havoc.

There are two basic types of doubt that need to be distinguished. First, there is *minor doubt*. Minor doubt is the questioning and uncertainty that we carry along as we actively investigate an important spiritual issue. It is a common experience even among mature, knowledgeable believers. If minor doubt is a hindrance to prayer at all, it will likely be short lived. It is often seen as a sign of growth in believers when they have minor doubts. These are doubts that often propel people to dig more deeply into God's Word, seek advice from wise people, and uncover answers to the questions that trouble them. Rather than being debilitating, minor doubt can be a pathway of growth and greater knowledge.

Serious doubt, however, is a different species. If someone has trouble maintaining belief in God, or has deep misgivings that Jesus really did rise from the dead, that is going to have a profound effect on going to God in prayer or believing that he would answer such things.

Compare a person with serious doubt to someone who is confident in his knowledge about the arguments for and against God's existence and thinks that the positive case for

God is so strong that he is utterly compelled to believe in God. Or consider someone who has studied the historical record about Jesus and thinks that the resurrection is true beyond a reasonable doubt, indeed, that it is one of the best-attested facts of the ancient world. Do you think a Christian who has that level of knowledge and conviction that these essential teachings are true will go to God with greater trust and expectation that God will hear and respond than someone who is racked with serious doubt? Of course, the answer is yes. Serious doubts about the essentials of Christian doctrine can be debilitating for prayer, as well as other spiritual disciplines.

Minor doubts we can weather. After all, we all have them at some point for various reasons, and often they help us develop stronger convictions as we discover new answers and have a broader understanding of life in general. Harboring serious doubts, however, is simply not going to be a foundation for a life of prayer, especially a vibrant one.

But you would be surprised to know how many people there are in our churches who go through the Christian motions but harbor deep within their souls serious doubts about the central teachings of Christianity. Hence their relationship with God and their prayer life suffers dramatically.

It does not have to be that way. I am convinced that a

deeper knowledge of the reality of essential Christian claims and doctrines is right at our fingertips. As I said before, God was generous in providing us evidence and good reasons to know him and to trust him. And a deeper, more robust prayer life will be one of the benefits of drinking deeply at this well of Christian knowledge.

OF COURSE GOD EXISTS

Over the last several decades a movement in the Western world called "the new atheism" has dominated a good deal of the discussion about God. It has been led by a handful of scientists, philosophers, and public thinkers who have gained a substantial following. And, of course, these "new atheists" and their followers are quite certain that God does not exist (which I assume annoys God a great deal).

But the new atheists are just dead wrong on this. I know it's not polite to say someone is dead wrong on something, but in some cases you just have to call it like it is. And besides, there is good biblical precedent for doing so: "The fool says in his heart, 'There is no God'" (Psalm 14:1).

On occasion, a position is so indefensible that it implodes upon even the most preliminary analysis. This is the case with atheism. As some of the best Christian philosophers have demonstrated, atheists, even to begin to make their case against God, have to utilize key ideas derived from theism. They lose even before they get started. Truth, knowledge, logic, reason, and the very ability to think about these concepts are all tools an atheist must use to make his case. But these are tools that can come only from God in the first place. So if the atheist wants to argue against God, he must grab and use tools provided by God. This would be like using your computer to type out an argument that electricity is a myth.

I have a significant advantage in being able to speak to this issue because I have been the editor of one of the top academic journals in this field for over twenty years. And we have read and published hundreds of high-level articles on God's existence and closely related topics. If there were some new commanding argument against God or in favor of atheism, I would have encountered it. But there is nothing compelling, nothing whatsoever that would justify these new atheists in their "certain" conclusions against God. Indeed, everything seems stacked against them from start to finish. Although I can't give detailed arguments here, let me summarize just a few of the most relevant points.

Why is there something rather than nothing? Try as they might, secular philosophers have made no progress whatsoever on this, the most fundamental question of philosophy and science. Christian thinkers and philosophers point out that if it is reasonable to believe that God exists (and it is), this question is answered. Something exists because a powerful, eternal, loving God willed it to be so and brought it all into being for his purposes.

The beginning of the universe. The overwhelmingly dominant view in science and philosophy is that the universe began to exist (in other words, it has not always been here). Since the universe had a beginning, it follows tightly that there was an immensely powerful personal being who got it all going in the first place—and that being is God. There simply are no other reasonable options.

Consciousness. When we see the order and intelligibility of the universe, we are aware of it because of our consciousness. But the consciousness we possess is not a feature of the building blocks or components of the physical universe (rocks, stars, space, hydrogen, quarks). How did humans (and animals) acquire consciousness from a universe that does not contain it or have any plausible means to generate it? Answer: it did not come from the physical universe. Rather, God, who is himself a conscious being, is the source of our consciousness. Even atheists must use their consciousness, which cannot be derived from a godless universe, to argue against God.

Information. Living things have DNA. DNA is a vast complex library of information. Coherent information does not occur without intelligence or mind. If there is no personal God, and all that exists is matter, energy, time, and blind chance, then there is no source of intelligence, mind, and information. An intelligent God must exist as a source of the information and intelligence in the universe.

Morality. We are moral creatures. We have a deep sense of right and wrong even if some of us have broken moral compasses. And again, if the only elements at the foundation of our universe are matter, energy, time, and blind chance, where in the world did we get this deeply ingrained moral outlook? Answer: from God, a profoundly moral being who wrote his moral law on our hearts. Atheists argue all the time that bad things happening in the world count against a good God's existence. But from where exactly did the atheist get his concept of bad and good? You don't derive these moral categories from a universe that only has matter, space, time, energy, and random chance as its properties. Even the atheist must utilize that which comes from God (moral ideas) to argue against God.

Miracles. Miracles happen. In fact, they are abundant and well documented. (I know this sounds crazy if you are an atheist, but you need to get outside the atheist bubble more often and investigate the claims and the evidence—it is quite remarkable.) Without getting too philosophical, a miracle is an event for which the only adequate explanation is the direct and extraordinary intervention of God. If miracles occur (and they do), then God exists. Atheism holds to a universe that is completely explicable using the laws of chemistry and physics alone—no God necessary. But the existence of legitimate supernatural events (miracles) refutes that and points directly to a powerful being who stands above the laws of the physical sciences.

This brief list provides a glimpse of the intellectual problems atheism faces. And this is just a sample. In a book titled the *Handbook of Christian Apologetics*, the authors set forth *twenty* arguments for the existence of God. Each argument poses a nearly insurmountable challenge to atheism—and there are many more beyond those twenty.

Atheism is not true. The evidence and good reasoning is on the side of those who argue for God. Although the "new atheist" movement captured a large following, reason was never on their side. And I think the apostle Paul had an accurate take on why when he wrote Romans 1:19-21.

> What may be known about God is plain to them, because God has made it plain to them. For

since the creation of the world God's invisible qualities—his eternal power and divine nature—have been clearly seen, being understood from what has been made, so that people are without excuse.

For although they knew God, they neither glorified him as God nor gave thanks to him, but their thinking became futile and their foolish hearts were darkened.

God exists. You can be sure of that. He wants us to *know* that he exists and not just hope or wish that he exists. That's why he left so many clear signposts pointing in his direction. Moreover, he also wants us to *know* that he is a loving heavenly Father who delights in hearing our needs and responding to our requests.

THE EXTRAORDINARY CLAIMS ABOUT JESUS

Another area of doubt that can derail fervent prayer and Christian commitment is misgivings about the person and work of Jesus. The New Testament teaches that Jesus is God in human flesh, the savior of humankind, and the one who conquered death on our behalf. And for our purpose in this study, he is also the one who spoke the words I am focusing on in chapter 15 of the Gospel of John.

During my academic career I've interacted with scholars who have a wide range of opinions on Jesus. A few think Jesus never actually existed. Some believe Jesus was a wise sage who was able to meet people's emotional needs, but not much more. Some think Jesus was a political radical who, rightly or wrongly, got himself crucified by the Romans. I've even met one who thinks Jesus was some sort of space alien beamed down to earth from the mother ship.

There seems to be an endless stream of opinion about the life and work of Jesus of Nazareth—unless, of course, you set aside your preconceived ideas and take the historical record seriously. If you do this, then a clear and persistent picture of Jesus comes forth. And it is a picture that cannot help but command our unwavering attention. The Jesus who emerges from the ancient scrolls and the parchments truly can unlock the most significant mysteries of our existence, including the enduring mysteries of death and eternal life.

There is a significant group of scholars who dig deeply into these raw historical sources about Jesus, and are convinced that Jesus was a real person, claimed to be God, and came back from the dead three days after being crucified in first-century Jerusalem, exactly as the New Testament describes. The weight of the historical record is with this group of scholars. We have excellent reason to believe that the resurrection of Jesus was a knowable historical event to which all the best evidence points.

The resurrection of Jesus really is the key to everything that is eternally meaningful. If there is solid historical reason to believe that Jesus rose from the dead, it confirms that he existed and that he was not just a sage or a revolutionary. But the reality of the resurrection does much more than that. During his ministry Jesus claimed to be God and he claimed he was going to die for the sins of the world. If he did indeed come back from the dead, as he predicted he would, we then have excellent reason to believe these two crucial claims. And we also have excellent reason to believe one more important claim: that those of us who put our trust in him will likewise live forever.

THE CASE FOR JESUS'S
CONQUEST OF DEATH

There are two rather remarkable things about the evidence that surrounds the resurrection of Jesus. First, there is so much of it, especially when compared to other events in ancient history. And second, so many scholars of very diverse opinions agree on so many of the basic facts.

One of the world's top experts on the resurrection of Jesus, Dr. Gary Habermas, did a comprehensive study of what scholars around the world have said about the basic facts of the case.[1] Many of these scholars are not believers. Indeed, many of them are neutral on the matter or have concluded that Jesus was not the Son of God and did not come back from the dead. This is important to know so that we can be confident that Habermas's work is not stacking the historical deck in favor of the resurrection. So when the full range of scholars is consulted—whether they are believers or not—what they have in common with regard to the historical details is extraordinary.

Habermas compiled a range of facts that "virtually all scholars who research this area" think are historically true. Habermas and others are right in calling these facts "historical bedrock"—reliable data that could be used in a courtroom, the science lab, or the historian's library to formulate confident conclusions. So just what are these facts that virtually all scholars agree on? Well, here is a brief list accompanied by a few of my comments.

Jesus died by Roman crucifixion. This is a bedrock fact on which scholars who do research in this area agree (and this is true for all the facts I list after this). Since it is a solid fact that Jesus died, then it is also a solid fact that he was a real historical figure. Those who say he is not (and you will find them on the Internet) are well outside the margins of legitimate historical research. This fact also puts to rest the idea that Jesus did not *die* on the cross but rather fainted, was taken for dead, and later regained strength. Modern research into ancient crucifixion practices makes it abundantly clear that Jesus experienced a certain death at the hands of a Roman execution team.

He was buried, most likely in a private tomb. Criminals would most often be thrown into a common pit grave, so Jesus's body being placed in a private tomb is something special. Some scholars go even further, saying that it was not just a private tomb but a rock-hewn burial cave owned by Joseph of Arimathea, a member of the Sanhedrin in Jerusalem—exactly as described in the New Testament.

Soon afterward, the disciples were discouraged, bereaved, and despondent, having lost hope. This fact confirms that Jesus did indeed have close followers and that they were devastated by his death. It also reaffirms that Jesus *died* by crucifixion.

Jesus's tomb was found empty soon after his body was placed there. Even though it wins agreement among scholars, this fact is wrestled over the most. And I think we can see why. If it is historical bedrock that Jesus's tomb was found empty just a few days after his burial, this is an astonishing corroboration of a key detail in the resurrection accounts in the Gospels. The empty tomb now has to be explained in order for skeptics to hold on to their naturalistic theories. But if Jesus really did rise from the dead, the empty tomb has an immediate explanation.

The disciples had experiences that they believed were actual appearances of the risen Jesus. The historical sources are quite strong on this point, so I can see why more than one prominent atheist scholar agrees with this fact. Multiple witnesses claim that they saw Jesus alive after his death by crucifixion. I find it extraordinary that this is confirmed by a strong consensus of modern scholars. But the next one may be the best of all.

Due to these experiences, the disciples' lives were thoroughly transformed. They were even willing to die for this belief. This is a tremendously powerful fact in support of the resurrection of Jesus. Not only did the disciples really think they saw him alive again, but they were transformed in some profound way to the point of being willing to give up their lives rather than disavow this testimony. I cannot think of anything plausible that could trigger such a weighty inward change apart from the disciples encountering Jesus alive again, risen from the grave.

Now, it is true that people die for all kinds of things they *believe* to be true but aren't (think Muslim terrorists or kamikaze pilots). Is this what happened with the disciples? No, their case is quite different from someone who dies for a belief that turns out to be wrong. The disciples were in a special position to *know* the truth of the situation. If Jesus were still dead, they would know it. If he were alive again, they would know that. They weren't acting on belief but on certain knowledge. They would not have given their lives for something they *knew* to be untrue. And to claim that they did defies both reason and ordinary human behavior. No, the only plausible explanation is that they really saw Jesus alive again and acted upon it by going throughout the Mediterranean region proclaiming this fact. And when threatened with death, they did not recant, because they were acting on *knowledge* and not mere belief.

There are a good number of other points of evidence thought to be bedrock facts by the scholarly community that provide solid support for the bodily resurrection of Jesus. For example, James (the brother of Jesus) was a skeptic who was converted to the faith when he believed he saw the risen Jesus. Likewise, Saul (Paul), a persecutor of Christ followers, came to faith when he also believed he saw the risen Jesus.

In the face of a solid set of facts like those above that are agreed upon by a diverse group of investigators (a rare situation in any human endeavor), the next step for a good scientist or courtroom lawyer is to find a theory that captures all the facts and provides the very best explanation. Skeptical scholars have tried out a variety of theories: the legend theory, the swoon (fainting) theory, the hallucination theory, the wrong tomb theory, and even the identical twin theory! None of these theories do justice to the facts of the case. All have giant holes in them with regard to explaining all the bedrock data.

But there is a theory that captures every single data point: Jesus came back from the dead in his own body exactly as the New Testament describes. The historical record provides us with all the justification we need to proclaim the same thing that the closest followers of Jesus began proclaiming on the first Easter Sunday. Hallelujah, he is risen, he is risen indeed!

CONFIDENCE AND KNOWLEDGE
AS THE FOUNDATION

I hope it is becoming clear why I have included a chapter on apologetics (reasons for faith) in a book devoted to a teaching of Jesus on petitionary prayer. It is crucial that we have confidence in the fact that a personal God exists and that he loves us and hears us. We need to know that Jesus died for our sins and clothed us in righteousness so that we can confidently approach God with our needs. We need to know that everything we do in this brief life will carry eternal weight because, if we have trusted him for our salvation, we will live forever.

If we have serious doubts about God's existence or the deity and work of his Son, Jesus, we will not be particularly useful to God in the kingdom work to which he has called us. The Lord's important work will have significant trouble being accomplished through us if we are not confident in the basic teachings of Scripture.

"Blind faith" is not where our strength lies. Rather, our strength will come through the awesome foundation of *knowledge* that God, by his grace, provided for us. He wants us to *know*. If you want to live big for Jesus, if you want to share your faith effectively, and if you want your prayers to be heard and to shake the foundations, then you need to be confident that the gospel is objectively true. As it says in Hebrews 11:6, "Anyone who comes to [God] must believe that he exists and that he rewards those who earnestly seek him."

CHAPTER 5

I Am the Vine and You Are the Branches

This whole book centers on what the Lord Jesus Christ said in John 15:7—"Ask whatever you wish, and it will be done for you." But before we can effectively dig into those exact words, we need to know something about the context of the passage.

Reading passages of the Bible in context is very important. A lot of mistakes are made when people take one verse of the Bible and think that it was designed to stand by itself. It was not. Each word, sentence, paragraph, and chapter is part of a larger message that needs to be considered in a proper interpretation. So let's look at the big picture to see what John 15:7 says in its context.

THE FOURTH GOSPEL

We find this verse in the book of John, one of the historically reliable accounts of the life of Jesus that we call Gospels. The book was written by a man named John who was one of the twelve disciples, or students, who were with Jesus for almost his entire public ministry in the land of Israel. So John had a front-row seat to almost all of what Jesus said or did during that time. He was even part of the inner circle of three who got to see some very special things that the other nine disciples did not.

John's brief biography covers only about three years of Jesus's life on earth. He begins with Jesus as an adult meeting John the Baptist, who baptizes Jesus and calls him the "Lamb of God, who takes away the sin of the world" (John 1:29), which was Jesus's primary calling. He ends with Jesus's death on the cross, his resurrection from the dead, and several postresurrection appearances.

When we arrive at chapter 15, where our text is found, we are already near the end of the story. In his account, John lingers on the last hours of Jesus's life. Nearly one-third of his Gospel covers this period. It would be easy to imagine this because those hours would have been seared into John's mind in a special way for the rest of his life. Trauma can stamp vivid memories onto the psyche. Witnessing or being nearby the personal agony, painful prayers, the arrest, the trials, the violent scourging, the innocent Jesus dying slowly on a Roman cross—and then hiding in fear for your life—was maximally distressing. And it would have been more so for people like the disciples who had the most profound hope that Jesus would take the throne of Israel and replace both the Romans and the corrupt religious establishment.

So the final teaching times, those surrounding such deep pain and disappointment, were not something that John could or would forget. In addition, earlier on that very same night, Jesus promised his disciples that the Holy Spirit would come to comfort them and remind them of everything Jesus had said to them (John 14:26).

LAST-STRAW LAZARUS

Chapters 11 through 14 of John's Gospel set the stage. Jesus is feared and despised by most of the religious leaders in Jerusalem. Indeed, they had wanted for a long time to remove Jesus from the scene. But Jesus was popular with the people, so the leaders had to be careful. The deadly antagonism they had toward Jesus reached a crescendo when Jesus performed an over-the-top miracle just two miles down the road from Jerusalem. The news of this provocative event would spread like wildfire.

A dear friend of Jesus, a man named Lazarus, tragically died. He had been dead for several days when Jesus finally arrived on the scene. Jesus sorrowfully greeted the mourning family and friends, and then had them assemble with him at the tomb. After a brief prayer that all could hear, Jesus spoke the command, "Lazarus, come out!" (John 11:43). Lazarus then walked out of the tomb with his grave clothes still on, got cleaned up, and then resumed living a normal life.

Can you imagine something like this in our day? The phrase "melting the Internet" would not even come close to capturing the global messaging tsunami that would ensue.

The religious leaders in Jerusalem heard the news about Lazarus in no time and soon thereafter met to plot the arrest and death of Jesus. It had all gone too far. They could no longer ignore Jesus. If he kept teaching and performing signs and wonders among the people, he could eventually foment an intervention by the Roman government. And this was unthinkable for the Jewish leaders. It had the potential to diminish or completely remove them from their positions of power.

After lying low for several days, Jesus and the Twelve entered Jerusalem. Word got around quickly that Jesus was coming toward the city. Throngs of pilgrims were in the area for the Passover Festival. The curious, the needy, the hopeful, and the overly exuberant lined the streets. And as Jesus passed, they waved palm branches and, filled with messianic hope, shouted the very dangerous words, "Blessed is the king of Israel!" As you might expect, this only inflamed the fears of the religious leaders, who doubled down on their plan to eliminate the threat.

At the end of John 12, Jesus predicts his own death to his confused followers. Chapters 13 and 14 record Jesus trying to comfort and prepare his disciples for what awaits him. The foot washing, the Last Supper, the promise of the Holy Spirit, and honest, difficult dialogue took place at their last evening together in the upper room. The last words of chapter 14 are those of Jesus, "Come now; let us leave."

INTO THE NIGHT

This is where chapter 15 begins. The eleven disciples (only eleven now because Judas Iscariot had already left to betray the Lord) followed Jesus out into a cool spring evening still bathed in late sunlight. Soon the full moon of the Passover would light their way. The text does not say what exactly their route was, but it would not be long before they all arrived in the Garden of Gethsemane facing an armed mob sent from the chief priests and religious leaders.

On the way, they almost certainly passed the temple. According to the ancient Jewish historian Josephus, on the front of the temple was a decorative "golden vine with grape clusters hanging from it, a marvel of size and artistry." Some of the grape clusters were "the height of a man." They then crossed the Kidron Valley and began to climb the Mount of Olives upon which were planted olive tree groves and vineyards. Some scholars believe that Jesus was teaching as they walked. Time was short, and he still had much he wanted to say to them. When they passed one of the many vineyards, Jesus likely stopped and began a new lesson.

THE OBJECT LESSON

Jesus is famous for his use of metaphors, stories, and object lessons. In a day when there was no PowerPoint, using a familiar object to illustrate an idea was a great memory tool. He was probably pointing to one of the grape plants on the side of the road—an object as familiar to people in that day as anything in their day-to-day lives could be. No one was going to miss the metaphor. Growing grapes was literally as old as the hills. Noah planted and tended a vineyard as soon as he emerged from the ark. Ancient Greek civilization had Dionysus, god of the grape harvest and wine. Archaeology has revealed pictographs in ancient Egyptian tombs showing careful cultivation of vineyards 2,500 years before the birth of Christ.

The planting, growing, and care of grapevines, today called "viticulture," has changed little over the centuries. Grapes are the most widely grown fruit in the world. And even today grapes are central to Israel's agriculture and economy. It would be hard to find a more timeless metaphor for a key spiritual lesson everyone would be familiar with in Jesus's day and beyond.

The lesson Jesus taught, though, was anything but business as usual.

John 15:1-8

> I am the true vine, and my Father is the gardener. [2] He cuts off every branch in me that bears no fruit, while every branch that does bear fruit he prunes so that it will be even more fruitful. [3] You are already clean because of the word I have spoken to you. [4] Remain in me, as I also remain in you. No branch can bear fruit by itself; it must remain in the vine. Neither can you bear fruit unless you remain in me.

⁵I am the vine; you are the branches. If you remain in me and I in you, you will bear much fruit; apart from me you can do nothing. ⁶If you do not remain in me, you are like a branch that is thrown away and withers; such branches are picked up, thrown into the fire and burned. ⁷If you remain in me and my words remain in you, ask whatever you wish, and it will be done for you. ⁸This is to my Father's glory, that you bear much fruit, showing yourselves to be my disciples.

THE TRUE VINE

Jesus starts his teaching in John 15 with the last of the seven great "I am" sayings in John's Gospel—I am the bread of life, I am the light of the world, I am the good shepherd, and so on. These sayings carry deep theological meaning that amplify in subtle ways Jesus's claim to be God in human flesh. In John 15:1 the "I am" construction also amplifies his claim to be the "true vine," which turns out to be a vigorous word picture. In the Old Testament, the nation of Israel was often referred to as the vine, and the people of Israel consciously identified with that image. That is why the vine of gold was on the entrance to the temple and why the vine was used on ancient coins in the land to represent Israel.

However, the Old Testament identification with the vine turned out not to be a positive one for Israel. A well-tended vineyard could produce wonderful fruit—a symbol of faithfulness, obedience, and prosperity in the Lord. But the people of Israel were over and over again unfaithful to God. They are thus represented by a vine that produces no fruit or only rotten fruit. Take, for instance, the "song of the vineyard" in the book of Isaiah: "My loved one had a vineyard on a fertile hillside…He looked for a crop of good grapes, but it yielded only bad fruit…And he looked for justice, but saw bloodshed; for righteousness, but heard cries of distress" (5:1,2,7). These laments are repeated in Ezekiel, Jeremiah, and the Psalms. Israel is a vine all right, but a fruitless vine, wild and rebellious, that has been unfaithful and has gone its own way.

It is against this background that Jesus says he is the "true vine." Unlike ancient Israel, Jesus is in close communion, obedience, and faithfulness to the Father. He is capable of producing good fruit and, indeed, is the source of all good fruit.

THE BRANCHES

Jesus expands the metaphor a few verses later by calling his followers "the branches." Jesus, the master, is the vine.

We, his students, are the branches. Given modern terminology this can be a bit confusing. When we think of a vine, we think of something Tarzan swings on, or a slender stem that can climb or that creeps along the ground and extends far from the base of the plant.

When Jesus says he is the vine, he is painting a different picture. What Jesus, and the culture of the day, meant by *vine* was the hearty base of the grape plant. These would be the large, heavy parts of the plant that remain during the dormant season in the fall and winter months—after all the spring growth of branches, shoots, leaves, and fruit had been trimmed off. This base is made up of the rootstock, the trunk, the head, and the cordons of the grape plant. In Jesus's definition, these parts all make up the vine—the solid, woody, perennial anatomy of the plant that remains and forms the foundation for grape production year after year.

The *branches* in Jesus's definition are the new shoots (called *canes* after a year of growth) that run along the trellis strings and directly hold all the clusters of grapes in the spring and summer, and then are removed or pruned back after the growing season.

One does not need to be an expert in the details of plant anatomy to get Jesus's message. It is very simple. He is the vine—that is, he is the perennial base that draws up all the water and nutrients from the soil and sends them out to the branches (us) to provide everything we need to bear fruit. If we are properly plugged into him, then we are ready. Fruit production will be inevitable.

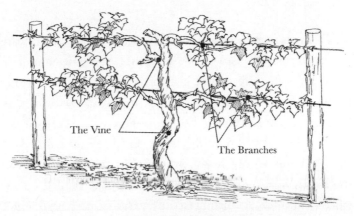

The Vine

The Branches

This illustration adapted by Maggie Hazen for this book.

The Father is the gardener or vinedresser who trims, cultivates, and shapes the plant with the goal of maximizing quality and quantity of fruit production. He oversees the vineyard because it belongs to him. He knows about everything that goes on in there. And just as the Father gave every opportunity for the ancient nation of Israel to bear fruit and expected them to do so, he gives us the same opportunity to bear fruit for him with great expectation.

CUTTING

> He cuts off every branch in me that bears no
> fruit, while every branch that does bear fruit
> he prunes so that it will be even more fruitful
> (John 15:2).

This verse captures some vital but simple spiritual meaning in the daily business of the Father, the gardener. The main message here is that just as the actual branch needs to be attached to the main vine in order to bear clusters of grapes, so we need to be plugged into Jesus if we want to have any hope of bearing God's good fruit. And the gardener wisely removes branches that are not bearing fruit. What good are they for the business of the vineyard? And since, according to the text, all branches attached to the "true vine" will bear fruit of some kind, there are commentators who think that the branches that are not bearing fruit represent unbelievers who appear to be followers of Jesus but are not. Judas Iscariot—who, at the very moment Jesus is speaking these words, is busy betraying his master—would be a prime example. Judas experienced everything the other disciples did, but in the end bore no fruit and was cut off.

PRUNING

But every branch that does bear fruit can expect to be pruned in order to bear more and better fruit. If we are bearing fruit, the expert gardener will prune us, shape us, and perfect us so that our yield will grow.

In viticulture, pruning is essential to healthy plants and abundant fruit production. In spring and summer, when fruit is actually growing on the plant, pruning is effective at getting better sun, airflow, and room for the grape clusters in the fast-growing canes and shoots. Pruning also focuses the plant's energies on fruit production rather than on tendrils, water sprouts, suckers, and foliage. Pruning helps keep disease from affecting the rest of the plant because bad leaves and shoots can be removed. And plant sickness is most likely to generate and spread in dense foliage that has not been pruned. (It's worth meditating on all these benefits of pruning. Vineyards, both ancient and new, are ripe with spiritual analogies.)

Now pruning in any human context sounds painful. When using this word as an analogy to spiritual growth and character development, it does not sound like an exciting part of the Christian life. Rather, it reminds us of personal discomfort in many forms. But spiritual pruning is going to happen with every believer who wants to grow in the Lord—and we shouldn't let the idea of pruning strike fear in us. Consider these things.

God loves us. He loves us more than we know. If you had a wise and deeply loving parent who wanted only the best for you growing up and was willing to discipline you to build your character and obedience, then you already have a clear picture of how the Father's pruning will affect us.

Fruit bearing is a glorious experience. If you have ever led someone to Christ; if you have delivered godly wisdom to someone profoundly confused about the direction of his life; if you have performed music that moved an entire auditorium to the heights of worship; if you have financed a successful missionary effort; if you have used any of your gifts to do the work of God and further his kingdom, then you know that the correction, discipline, or affliction you had to endure to get there were nothing compared to the joy of serving God with the highest skill and effectiveness. After witnessing the suffering that takes place in childbirth, most of us males are amazed that any woman would ever volunteer for it again. But the joy of love and new life keeps mothers going back for more. The same is true with the pruning that leads to the glory of fruit bearing in our lives.

It is preparation for eternity. It is not just about bearing fruit in this life. It is also about preparation for eternity with God. The apostle Paul saw a quantity and an intensity of pruning and pain that few Christians will ever experience. Yet he didn't hesitate to write, "Therefore we do not lose heart. Though outwardly we are wasting away, yet inwardly we are being renewed day by day. For our light and momentary troubles are achieving for us an eternal glory that far outweighs them all" (2 Corinthians 4:16-17).

We are comforted through pruning. If we are going through trouble or pain supervised by the vine grower himself, we can bet there are others in Christ who know how to comfort the afflicted. If there are people in our churches who bear fruit for the Lord, it is a sure thing that they have been through pruning. And they are the best ones to help us through the ordeal. God prunes us with one hand, and then provides comfort to us through his servants with the other hand.

Not all pruning is painful. When we think of pruning, we think of pruning shears digging into the wood and flesh of a plant with a cracking noise and a final *snap* as a chunk of the plant pinwheels through the air. Thinking too long about it reminds me of a gruesome movie scene I saw in which a mobster held pruning shears to the base of a man's pinky. That is not what we are talking about in the usual pruning at the hands of our loving gardener.

To be sure, pruning is removing the growth on a plant that will impede fruit production. But when I watched an expert vine keeper care for a row of vines one day, I learned an important lesson. He did not have pruning shears with him or anything sharp at all. He simply reached into the denser foliage and started snapping off leaves and unhelpful growth with his bare hands. It was fast, effective, and immediately improved the plant's ability to generate fruit. If plants could feel pain, this was about as small a dose as I could imagine that would produce an immediate and positive effect on fruit bearing.

By analogy, when I was a young Christian I went to a Bible study and prayer group that was attended by some devout and fervent young Christian men. I remember one meeting where several of them were facedown on the floor begging God in prayer to "be thorough with them." It was as if they were begging the gardener to get out the biggest, sharpest tools with which to carve on them. After witnessing this, I consciously took a different tack. I started praying, "God, help me learn your lessons the easy way as often as I can." Someone later pointed out to me that praying like this was simply a different way of asking God for wisdom. It was a prayer to hear God's Word, to trust it, and put it into practice without delay. Now there have been times when God has had to dig deeper and let me go through painful times to correct me, discipline me, and build my character. But he has been tremendously faithful in answering my prayer and showing me the more direct, less painful path to his will on most occasions.

As one commentator on this passage wrote, "God's 'pruning' is his gracious way of directing the flow of spiritual energy in order that his plans for our lives will be realized. While pruning is painful, it serves the necessary purpose of removing those branches that would otherwise absorb our time and energy in unproductive pursuits."[1]

YOU ARE ALREADY CLEAN

> You are already clean because of the word I have spoken to you (John 15:3).

It is a bit cryptic for Jesus to say, "You are already clean" at this point in his discourse. It seems like a sudden diversion from the vineyard metaphor. But looking at the Greek words being translated gives us more information. The Greek word translated "clean" (or "cleansed") is the same Greek word for "pruned." So one could read it as Jesus saying to the eleven disciples, "You have already been pruned and hence ready to bear fruit."

But using "clean," as most translators do, makes sense on several levels. First, pruning a branch during peak growing season, as I have already described, is quick, barehanded work of snapping off soft extraneous shoots. In our modern parlance, this kind of pruning could easily be considered "clean-up" work. Second, just hours earlier Jesus had washed the disciples' feet and said to them, "Those who have had a bath need only to wash their feet; their whole body is clean. And you are clean, though not every one of you" (John 13:10). By contrasting the disciples with Judas during the foot washing, Jesus was emphasizing not physical cleanliness by water, but spiritual purity. He is likely doing the same in 15:3.

Jesus then says that the disciples are clean "because of the word I have spoken to you." The term "word" here in Greek is *logos*. It denotes not just individual words or sayings but an entire body of teaching, a whole school of thought, a full collection of transformative thinking presented by Jesus through word and deed over their three years together. Jesus says the disciples are clean, not because of a physical washing or pruning, but rather by hearing and believing the full message of the Savior.

Years later the apostle Paul referred to this same change of heart and mind when someone is enveloped in the person and the teachings of the Lord Jesus: "Do not conform to the pattern of this world, but be transformed by the renewing of your mind. Then you will be able to test and approve what God's will is—his good, pleasing and perfect will" (Romans 12:2).

The disciples had heard and believed Jesus during their time with him, and Jesus affirms that with his declaration. The disciples were still confused and unclear on many things, and in just a few hours they were going to run from Jesus and even deny him. Yet, Jesus declares them clean through the power of his *logos*—and hence prepared to bear significant fruit.

REMAIN IN ME

> Remain in me, as I also remain in you. No branch can bear fruit by itself; it must remain in the vine. Neither can you bear fruit unless you remain in me (John 15:4).

We are back now to the full vine-and-branch symbol. When Jesus said, "Remain in me," he was using command language (the imperative mood), and in this case not just a one-time command, but also an ongoing command. The Lord really wanted to make sure that this idea would stick.

Capital letters and an exclamation point might capture it best in print: REMAIN IN ME AND DON'T STOP! Why? Because not only will branches not bear fruit if they are not firmly connected to the vine, but they simply won't survive.

This is where Jesus becomes almost obsessive with the word "remain" (perhaps better translated "abide," Greek *meno*). It occurs ten times in the first eleven verses of this chapter. Given who is saying it, how he is saying it, and the circumstances for saying it, we would do well to let Jesus's emphasis on remaining or abiding capture our full attention. This is at the same time a passionate plea and a promise to his beloved students. Within hours they will be scattered, scared, and feeling all their hope drained away in a torrent. They needed this message drilled down deeply into their souls and locked in. They didn't grasp what lay ahead and how desperately they would need to be firmly grafted into the vine—for the next few hours and days, and then for the rest of their lives.

YOU CAN DO NOTHING

> I am the vine; you are the branches. If you remain
> in me and I in you, you will bear much fruit;
> apart from me you can do nothing (John 15:5).

Repetition is Jesus's teaching method for this last shot at communicating with his students. He is the vine; his disciples are the branches. They must remain in him to see fruit come forth.

Heard that before. Got it.

But then he throws in something new to raise their eyebrows. It is a brief phrase that seems wildly untrue, until one looks at it from the proper perspective: "Apart from me you can do nothing."

For rebellious humans used to doing it "my way," this seems patently false. On the face of it, it seems to us that we can breathe, walk, earn money, play ping-pong, reproduce, vacation, and socialize apart from Jesus. We witness it happening every day. There are unbelievers who live eighty-plus years without him. There are those who don't even think Jesus was a real historical figure, yet they seem capable of living long productive lives. However, a closer look at this statement reveals two important truths that clear up the confusion.

First, although Jesus may not look the part while standing on a dusty pathway on the Mount of Olives giving this talk, there is excellent reason to believe that he is exactly who he claims to be: the very Son of God, and the Creator and Sustainer of all things. If Jesus stopped exercising his sustaining power, all that exists would likely vaporize in an instant. Paul wrote in his epistle to the Colossians that Jesus "is before all things, and in him all things hold together" (1:17). Now, I don't think Jesus was alluding to this power to keep atoms from flying apart in his statement that "apart from me, you can do nothing." But it is important to keep in mind the kind of being we are talking about. Since he is the Creator and Sustainer of all life, on many levels we are truly dependent on him moment by moment.

Second, Jesus was not saying that people could do absolutely "no thing" apart from him. Rather, in the context of remaining or abiding in Jesus, he is saying we can do nothing to accomplish *things of an eternal, holy, and spiritually meaningful nature*. Apart from him, we are, in essence, dead men walking. We live an illusion in which we think that having business success, accomplished kids, a large retirement account, health, vigor, and an award-winning golf swing is doing something eminently valuable. As Jesus said in the parable of the rich fool, "'You fool! This very night your life will be demanded from you. Then who will get what you have prepared for yourself?' This is how it will be with whoever stores up things for themselves but is not rich toward God" (Luke 12:20-21). And the only things we can do that will be rich toward God are those things derived from our solid connection with the Lord. Apart from him we cannot do anything of eternal value.

It's not hard to see why Jesus was so passionate and emphatic about this message. If we miss this, we miss everything. If unbelievers never come to the vine, they will never know the Lord or his fruit. If believers don't connect with the vine, they will be cut off from the source of life. As Robert Mounce says in his commentary on this passage, "Cut off from Christ by an unwillingness to abide, the professing Christian will be unable to produce fruit or, for that matter, do anything of spiritual consequence."[2]

C.T. Studd was a world-renowned cricket player at Cambridge University in 1880. Remarkably, and stunning his significant fan base, at the age of twenty-four he gave up his dreams of athletic stardom. He had come to Christ under the preaching of D.L. Moody and wanted to make every moment of his life count for Christ. He wrote, "What is all the fame and flattery worth…when a man comes to face eternity? I know that cricket would not last, and honour would not last, and nothing in this world would last, but it is worthwhile living for the world to come. How could I spend the best years of my life in living for the honours of this world, when thousands of souls are perishing every day?"

Later in life he penned an inspirational poem familiar

to Christians around the world for generations. One of the stanzas is:

> Only one life, yes only one,
>   Soon will its fleeting hours be done;
> Then, in "that day" my Lord to meet,
>   And stand before His Judgment seat;
> Only one life, 'twill soon be past,
>   Only what's done for Christ will last.

He died on the mission field of disease at the age of seventy after serving for nearly fifty years on three continents.

Admitting that we are powerless apart from Jesus is considered weakness by the world. But in another reversal that so often characterizes the teaching of Christ, exactly the opposite is true. Our utter dependence on him is our great comfort, our strength, and our power.

I do a great deal of public speaking, and before getting up in front of an audience, large or small, I always admit to God that "apart from you I can do nothing." I then ask for his blessing on my words and that my work will glorify him. I cannot recall a time that prayer has not been answered—even when I am in front of unbelieving, hostile audiences. I can't imagine going into hostile territory without being tightly connected to the vine. He is the true source of power—both for bearing fruit and for glorifying the Father. And admitting our complete and desperate need for him is one way of staying welded tightly to our godly source of success.

THE CARROT AND THE STICK

> If you do not remain in me, you are like a branch that is thrown away and withers; such branches are picked up, thrown into the fire and burned (John 15:6).

Jesus used the carrot and the stick to get his message across in this passage. (Although a carrot is not fruit, in the case of my analogy here, it is.) Those who experience the joy of the Lord through bearing his fruit know it is a powerful incentive to remain plugged in to Jesus. The delight of bearing fruit is the carrot that draws us forward in the Lord.

The stick to motivate us to abide in Jesus sounds ominous—thrown away, withers, thrown into the fire, burned. Some commentators see the symbols of judgment here and conclude that Jesus might be talking about losing one's salvation. Or it might be a reference to Judas Iscariot again as in verse 2. Judgment certainly seemed to visit Judas in that the guilt of his betrayal was so strong that he went out and hanged himself. That could line up with a branch that is thrown away, withers, and burns.

But some scholars caution against making too much of the symbols in this verse. It is, after all, a simile—a common literary device used often by Jesus to make colorful comparisons. "You are *like* a branch that is thrown away and withers." So we need to be careful in drawing major theological conclusions from an isolated illustration like this. The broadest and safest interpretation of this word picture is this: If we do not remain tightly connected with Jesus, it will be disastrous for our fruit bearing and for our overall spiritual life. It is another way of saying, "Apart from me you can do nothing." There might be more going on in this verse, but virtually everyone should be able to agree on the broad interpretation. The tasty carrot is the joy of bearing the Lord's fruit; the painful stick is the knowledge that if we do not remain in Jesus, we will be giving up any meaningful kingdom activity in our lives.

†

You are right if you are thinking, *Wait, he is concluding before he expounds on verse 7*. Verse 7 is my main focus, so I'm going to give it its own chapter. So let's move on to John 15:7.

CHAPTER 6

Wait, What Did He Say?—John 15:7

As I mentioned earlier, I had a bit of startle one time when I read John 15:7—"If you remain in me and my words remain in you, ask whatever you wish, and it will be done for you." I was plodding along reading the book of John, which I had done dozens of times, when the latter half of this verse struck me. What in the world was Jesus saying? Did he really mean it?

And it makes me wonder now how the disciples reacted when Jesus first spoke these words. There they were, walking slowly through a vineyard on a cool evening with the sun going down and the moon coming up, trying to take in all that Jesus was saying. What were they thinking?

It could be that they took these words in stride because

they had heard this basic idea on several occasions. Indeed, they had already heard it earlier that same evening when Jesus was teaching in the upper room.

> Very truly I tell you, whoever believes in me will do the works I have been doing, and they will do even greater things than these, because I am going to the Father. And I will do whatever you ask in my name, so that the Father may be glorified in the Son. You may ask me for anything in my name, and I will do it (John 14:12-14).

The disciples must have been paying attention as best they could because their teacher started off his message with "Very truly I tell you…" In essence he was saying, "Hey, everyone, do not miss what I am about to say!" And then he says it twice: "I will do whatever you ask in my name…You may ask for anything in my name, and I will do it." It's as if Jesus wanted to tattoo this promise on several parts of their bodies. They needed to hear it, feel it, and never forget it.

But it wasn't just about promised answers to prayer. In verse 12, Jesus also said that they would do the supernatural works that they had seen him do—*and even greater ones*. And we shouldn't forget that this was just a few days after they had seen Lazarus walk out of his tomb at Jesus's command. I'm guessing these ideas were simply too much to take in. It was like drinking from a large, forceful, and profound fire hose. No wonder Jesus promised the Holy Spirit would help them remember it all (John 14:26)—they were going to need divine assistance to log it all in.

THE MOST DIRECT ASK
AND RECEIVE PASSAGES

On several occasions during his extended ministry, Jesus had introduced the idea that we should expect answers to our prayers. These are recorded in all four Gospels.

After teaching on prayer and introducing the Lord's Prayer to his followers, Jesus said this as recorded in Matthew (see also Luke 11:1-13): "Ask and it will be given to you; seek and you will find; knock and the door will be opened to you. For everyone who asks receives; the one who seeks finds; and to the one who knocks, the door will be opened" (Matthew 7:7-8).

And then Jesus uses a rabbinic literary device found in both the Old and New Testaments to drive the point home. It is called arguing from the lesser to the greater: If *A* is true, how much more must *B* be true. We see this pattern in the following verses: "Which of you, if your son asks for bread, will give him a stone? Or if he asks for a fish, will give him a snake? If you, then, though you are evil, know how to give good gifts to your children, how much more will your Father in heaven give good gifts to those who ask him!" (Matthew 7:9-11).

The point is persuasive. If you sinful (evil) parents give good things to your children, *how much more* will an eternal, all-powerful being whose primary attribute is love give good gifts to meet the needs of those who ask, seek, and knock. Conclusion: It's a done deal; you should expect to receive what you have asked for.

Although it is not as tightly stated as the prayer promise we are highlighting in John 15, this passage clearly communicates God's tender love for us and his desire to give us good gifts. This expectation of good gifts in response to our prayers is an undeniable and essential element of the Christian life.

To add to our expectation of God's loving response to our prayers, let's look at a statement by Jesus found in Matthew 21:18-22. Jesus and his disciples were walking from a nearby town into Jerusalem when Jesus, in what looked like a random action, cursed a fig tree that was bearing no fruit. "Immediately," the text says, the tree "withered"—that is, it instantly shriveled up. The disciples were not in tune with the deeper symbolic meaning of the event at the time, they were simply amazed at the speedy response of the tree to Jesus's words. So they asked, "How did the fig tree wither so quickly?"

> Jesus replied, "Truly I tell you, if you have faith and do not doubt, not only can you do what was done to the fig tree, but also you can say to this mountain, 'Go, throw yourself into the sea,' and it will be done. If you believe, you will receive whatever you ask for in prayer" (Matthew 21:21-22, see also Mark 11:22-25).

Before we start looking for flying mountains, we need to know that "moving mountains" was a common metaphor in Jewish literature and in common speech at the time, as it is for us today for overcoming one's problems or major obstacles. Paul confirms this when he uses it in 1 Corinthians 13:2, "If I have a faith that can move mountains."

The simple way that the disciples would have heard this is:

- "Truly I tell you"—important truth coming
- "if you have faith and do not doubt"—if you trust God and know that he can deliver

- "fig tree"—small miracle
- "mountain"—big miracle
- "If you believe" (same word as faith)—if you trust God and you really think he can do it
- "you will receive whatever you ask for in prayer"—you will receive whatever you ask for in prayer

And the simple combined message is this: God is prepared to do amazing things in and through us, big and small, if we trust him and know in our minds and hearts that he can deliver whatever we ask for in prayer.

OTHER ASK AND RECEIVE PASSAGES

We find this same message in other parts of the New Testament outside the Gospels. Because it is a strong theme in John's Gospel, we would expect to find this theme mentioned in John's epistles too. And we do.

> Dear friends, if our hearts do not condemn us, we have confidence before God and receive from him anything we ask... (1 John 3:21).

This is the confidence we have in approaching

God: that if we ask anything according to his will, he hears us. And if we know that he hears us—whatever we ask—we know that we have what we asked of him (1 John 5:14-15).

And again, later in his Gospel, John records Jesus saying,

In that day you will no longer ask me anything. Very truly I tell you, my Father will give you whatever you ask in my name. Until now you have not asked for anything in my name. Ask and you will receive, and your joy will be complete (John 16:23-24).

The apostles Paul and James are not reluctant to put this theme on display either:

If God is for us, who can be against us? He who did not spare his own Son, but gave him up for us all—how will he not also, along with him, graciously give us all things? (Romans 8:31-32).

If any of you lacks wisdom, you should ask God, who gives generously to all without finding fault, and it will be given to you (James 1:5).

I am highlighting here only the most direct statements about how ready God is to hear our prayers and faithfully answer them. There are also dozens of passages that do this indirectly, showing us by example how God stands ready to give us what we ask for. Here are four samples.

> The prayer of a righteous person is powerful and effective. Elijah was a human being, even as we are. He prayed earnestly that it would not rain, and it did not rain on the land for three and a half years. Again he prayed, and the heavens gave rain, and the earth produced its crops (James 5:16-18).

> Peter was kept in prison, but the church was earnestly praying to God for him. The night before Herod was to bring him to trial, Peter was sleeping between two soldiers, bound with two chains, and sentries stood guard at the entrance. Suddenly an angel of the Lord appeared and a light shone in the cell. He struck Peter on the side and woke him up. "Quick, get up!" he said, and the chains fell off Peter's wrists...Peter followed him out of the prison...he went to the house of Mary the mother of John, also called Mark, where many people had gathered and were praying (Acts 12:5-12).

> In the morning, LORD, you hear my voice;

> in the morning I lay my requests before you
> and wait expectantly (Psalm 5:3).

> The Reubenites, the Gadites and the half-tribe
> of Manasseh…waged war against the Hagrites,
> Jetur, Naphish and Nodab. They were helped
> in fighting them, and God delivered the Hag-
> rites and all their allies into their hands, because
> they cried out to him during the battle. He
> answered their prayers, because they trusted in
> him (1 Chronicles 5:18-20).

It is against this consistent and prolific biblical backdrop of a God who faithfully responds to our prayers that we come back to John 15:7.

GOING DEEPER INTO JOHN 15:7

> If you remain in me and my words remain in
> you, ask whatever you wish, and it will be done
> for you.

It's obvious by now that I could have used other passages in the Bible to make my case that God loves to give us what we ask for in prayer. It is a clear biblical theme, and John 15:7 does a great job of capturing it.

Verse 7 starts out with a "double conditional," that is, two things need to be fulfilled before we see the result. First, we have to "remain" or "abide" in Jesus—nothing new there. It has already been mentioned five times in the previous six verses in this chapter of John. We as branches must remain continually plugged into the vine (Jesus) in order to be spiritually alive and in order to bear fruit.

Second, Jesus said, "If...my words remain in you..." This phrase is new to us and brings a fresh twist to the discourse. In verse 3 we heard Jesus say, "You are already clean because of the *word* I have spoken to you." And as I said in the previous chapter, this term "word" in Greek was *logos*. *Logos* was used to capture the whole body of Jesus's ministry and teaching. In verse 7 a different Greek term is translated "words" in the text. It is the word *rhemata* and it provides a subtle difference in the meaning.

In verse 3, the disciples are clean because of the *logos*. This is referring to their standing before Jesus and the Father. They had believed and trusted in Jesus and his salvation teachings (*logos*). They did not do this perfectly, of course, and that should give us comfort. After all, we do not believe his teachings or trust in him perfectly either. So there is hope for all who believe.

Verse 7 is not referring to the disciples' salvation standing before God, but rather their fitness for fruit bearing. In order to bear fruit, they must remain in Jesus and his words (*rhemata*) must remain in them. *Rhemata* refers here to the specific words or commands of Jesus that will empower the disciples to be obedient, to grow spiritually, to carry the gospel forward, and to pray in accord with the will of the Father. It is the same type of devotion to specific words from God that Jesus displays in his temptation in the wilderness. There the Lord said, "Man shall not live on bread alone, but on every word [*rhema*] that comes from the mouth of God" (Matthew 4:4).

The two conditions are perfectly designed to keep us plugged into Jesus the vine; he is our only source for spiritual life and fruit bearing. And his words are to abide in us, guiding us every step of the way. It is by his words that live in us that we will know what to ask of the Father in prayer.

None of this would raise much controversy among scholars, Bible teachers, and serious Bible readers. But then Jesus concludes with these perplexing words: "Ask whatever you wish, and it will be done for you."

DID JESUS REALLY MEAN THAT?

Did Jesus really mean what he packed into that last

clause? Are there other factors we're not taking into account? Are we understanding this correctly? This sounds too good to be true and it doesn't seem to match up with our experience. We have seen this abused by "faith" teachers. We don't want to build false hope in people. We don't want to look materialistic. We want to be realistic with our faith. We don't want to sound weird. We don't want to sound greedy. We want to make sure people don't have a bad view of Jesus.

Nevertheless, Jesus said it and we have to deal with it. (I find it ironic that a verse of immense promise, power, and generosity ends up causing us undue anxiety and confusion in our interpretive task!)

The reason I wanted to write this book is that I have seen an unnecessary lethargy and powerlessness in prayer. It is as if even serious Christians who know the Scriptures well spend far more time attempting to figure out why God *won't* answer prayer rather than focusing on how excited he is to hear our requests and give us what we ask for. They remind me of the old comic actor W.C. Fields when someone once caught him reading a Bible.

"Mr. Fields, what are you doing reading the Bible?"

"Well, I'm just looking for loopholes," Fields replied. "Just looking for loopholes."

When I talk to Christians about the prayer promise

of John 15:7, I'm continually amazed at how quickly they respond with doubt and suspicion. This has given me the sense that few Jesus-loving, Bible-reading Christians take these words of Jesus as seriously as they ought to. And if not, we might all be missing out on blessings, tools, and gifts that could take our ministries to a whole new level of power and impact.

Because the suspicion about verses like John 15:7 is so widespread—so many people looking for loopholes—I'm going to present and then respond to some of the skeptical notions offered up by our Christian brothers and sisters and by the culture at large.

CHAPTER 7

Death by a Thousand Qualifications

The Lord Jesus Christ encouraged us to pray. Indeed, he made it sound as though it could be a wonderful experience for those who do. It might actually be a source of great joy and delight.

Toward the end of his discourse on prayer in John 15, Jesus said, "I have told you this so that my joy may be in you and that your joy may be complete" (15:11). The psalmist wrote, "Take delight in the LORD, and he will give you the desires of your heart" (37:4). God speaks through the prophet Isaiah about his temple as a house of prayer for all: "These I will bring to my holy mountain and give them joy in my house of prayer" (56:7). And I find Jesus's words in Matthew 7:7 overflowing with joy, optimism, and expectation:

"Ask and it will be given to you; seek and you will find; knock and the door will be opened to you. For everyone who asks receives; the one who seeks finds; and to the one who knocks, the door will be opened."

However, some very fine Bible teachers today spend little time encouraging us in prayer the way the Lord did. The Lord emphasizes his willingness and joy in giving us what we ask for. Many Bible teachers, though, seem reluctant to mention that or emphasize it—even while it is a significant teaching theme of Jesus himself. These teachers see "petitionary" prayers that "ask" as unsophisticated and at the lower rungs of the spiritual ladder—maybe even taboo. In his book *Prayer*, Richard J. Foster noticed the same thing and wrote this about it:

> Some have suggested, for example, that while the less discerning will continue to appeal to God for aid, the real masters of the spiritual life go beyond petition to adoring God's essence with no needs or requests whatever. In this view our asking represents a more crude and naïve form of prayer, while adoration and contemplation are a more enlightened and high-minded approach, since they are free from any egocentric demands.

> This, I submit to you, is a false spirituality. Petitionary Prayer remains primary throughout our lives because we are forever dependent upon God. It is something we never really "get beyond," nor should we want to…The Bible itself is full of Petitionary Prayer and unabashedly recommends it to us.[1]

One comprehensive book on prayer by a dean of a major evangelical theology school did not have a single section devoted to asking God through petitionary prayer. He had nothing on the biblical case for asking God, what to ask God for, how to ask him, or the emphasis Jesus put on asking and asking persistently. Another book on prayer by a major pastoral figure in America had a small section on "asking" (how could one avoid it given the biblical emphasis on it), but this kind of petitionary prayer was qualified and diluted until it ended up on the bottom of the list of things we should consider while praying. In some instances, prayer even begins to look like a kind of divine drudgery—something we do because we are commanded to—rather than a source of peace, joy, and kingdom expectation. After reading some of these books, you would never suspect Jesus had ever said anything remotely like "Ask whatever you wish, and it will be done for you."

There is a strong sense in the modern church that asking God to meet some personal need, some family need, a ministry need, or to fulfill a personal desire for things like relationships or business success is ultimately beneath the mature Christian. Those requests are in some way selfish and miss the mark. Our main goals in prayer, they say, should be to examine oneself spiritually and grow in one's intimacy with God.

Now please don't get me wrong here. I love these books and these senior Christian teachers who emphasize prayer as a way to have a deeper connection with God. What they say is true, and I have learned much of great value from them. But their teaching often undervalues something that Jesus valued very highly: the overall power and benefit of petitionary prayer. By petitionary prayer I mean the kind of prayer that boldly asks God to meet our needs and our wants. And we have to find a way to bring this back into balance.

I won't dig deeply into why some teachers put petitionary prayer on the bottom shelf, but I will briefly mention three things I have noticed. First, it might be a reaction to our materialist age and how it has negatively affected the church. Prayer for things seems to play into this unhealthy materialistic appetite and hence muddies the pure water of prayer. Second, it might be a logical consequence of Reformed

(Calvinist) theology that has difficulty with the idea that asking in prayer can actually change the outcome of a situation already ordained by God. One way to solve that problem from a Reformed perspective is to deemphasize the "asking and receiving" part of prayer and instead to emphasize the meditative aspects and the inner spiritual communion with God. Third, more people than you might expect think petitionary prayer is in some way bothering God with unimportant matters.

I will leave it to others to sort out the causes in greater detail. But the effect of this kind of thinking is that we are missing out on much that the Lord wants us to have. Asking is key. It actually helps to form the kind of relationship that God wants to have with us—one in which we are deeply dependent on him. Remember what Jesus said in John 15:5? "Apart from me you can do nothing." So we ask and he responds. Charles Spurgeon summed it up well in a sermon over 130 years ago: "If you may have everything by asking in His Name, and nothing without asking, I beg you to see how absolutely vital prayer is."

Whether they are done consciously or not, one thing that the three moves listed above accomplish is this: It makes it so that the person does not have to deal with Jesus's provocative statement, "Ask whatever you wish, and it will be done for you." After all, if petitionary prayer stays on the bottom shelf, then we can effectively ignore Jesus's enthusiastic call to do it. Qualifications, objections, tortured interpretations, and redefinitions rule the day until the verse seems not to mean anything at all. Two philosophers in the 1950s called this treatment "death by a thousand qualifications." John 15:7 seems to have been killed off in the modern Christian mind in this way.

To demonstrate this, I have made a list of the explanations, clarifications, and objections that have been offered to get around the straightforward reading of this passage. Some are simplistic and some are naïve. Some are thoughtful and some are rather challenging. But all are qualifications or objections brought up by real people to help them dilute, dismiss, or reinterpret the provocative words of Jesus in John 15:7, "If you remain in me and my words remain in you, ask whatever you wish, and it will be done for you." So here they are along with my brief comments.

It is referring to stuff that happened way back when. This qualification tells us we shouldn't expect this verse to apply to us today. It was meant to apply only to what was taking place back in pristine Bible times. But this is a weak objection. There is no time stamp on these promises. In fact, in John 14:12, Jesus emphatically stated that "*whoever* believes in me will do the works I have been doing" (emphasis mine). And presumably "whoever" means anyone in their day or in future generations of believers.

"Well, ya need to be within spittin' distance of Jesus"—as one skeptic put it to me. He believed there was something special about being in spatial proximity to Jesus. It's an objection similar to the first one except it uses distance rather than time as a barrier. This man thought you had be close to the power source. There is no evidence for it, just this skeptic's feelings about it.

Jesus was speaking only to the disciples and hence it was meant only for them. This objection was answered in the first entry as well. Jesus said "whoever" meaning not just his immediate band of followers.

It was meant for a special class of Christian such as saints or official clergy. This qualification pops up mostly in bodies such as the Roman Catholic Church, where they have different ranks of ministry in the church. A Catholic would believe a priest or a saint might have special standing before God, but even Roman Catholic theology does not remove lay people from access to such promises as in John 15:7. We are back to "whoever" having access, as the text says.

It's an allegory and not meant to be taken literally. Actually there was a metaphor (not an allegory) in play in verses

1 through 6, but it ended at verse 6. Verse 7 is straight-forward talk from Jesus and free from metaphorical language. And we know that the disciples knew the difference. Just one chapter later (during the same evening discourse), Jesus said to the eleven, "Ask and you will receive, and your joy will be complete." Then, almost immediately afterward, the disciples said, "Now you are speaking clearly and without figures of speech" (John 16:24,29).

I'm a brand-new Christian; I doubt that what Jesus said applies to me. Actually, when I was a young Christian, this seemed to be the liveliest time of "asking and receiving" that I can remember. I, and many people I've spoken with over the years, remember fondly those early days of following Jesus. It was as if the Father wanted to show us how real he was and that he heard every word we spoke to him. I'm sure this is not a universal experience, but it is a common one. And I think it demonstrates that Jesus's promise applies to new believers even if they are not experts yet at abiding in Jesus and having his words abide in them.

I'm not much of a praying person. This isn't really a qualification, it is simply a formula for not having a relationship with God and missing out on opportunities to bear amazing fruit for the kingdom.

I tried it and it didn't work. In this passage we have the very Son of God telling us that if we abide in him and his words abide in us, we can ask for anything and it will be given to us. If it is not "working," it's not like a vacuum cleaner that needs a new fuse. It is a failure or setback in a relationship—and Jesus is not the responsible party. Anybody truly abiding in Jesus would not say, "I tried it and it didn't work." This objection reminds me of how the Christian thinker G.K. Chesterton responded to a charge from a colleague who said that Christianity was in some way deficient. "The Christian ideal has not been tried and found wanting," Chesterton said. "It has been found difficult and left untried."

The "qualifications" I've listed so far are real but almost frivolous. There are two qualifications, though, that are much more acute in their ability to kill off the promise of Jesus in John 15:7. I take these up next.

CHAPTER 8

From Abusing to Abiding

In my quest to find out why we do not believe this provocative prayer promise, I've had to ask myself, did Jesus really want us to hear him say over and over again, "Ask and you will receive," and then spend most of our time trying to figure out why we shouldn't believe his direct and emphatic words?

Scholarly commentators have actually done a very good job trying to understand what these passages mean and how they sync up with other passages of Scripture and the mature Christian life. But by the time they are done with their analyses, these "ask and receive" passages that are so prominent in the teaching of Jesus often end up getting pushed way out to the margins of our experience. We seem afraid of them, confused by them, or embarrassed about them. And our first thought doesn't seem to be to bask in the hope and joy these passages bring to us, but rather to explain them away or add qualifications as quickly as possible.

At this point I'd like to address the two most common barriers I have seen people run into in their attempt to fully accept a passage like John 15:7.

PASSAGES LIKE JOHN 15:7 ARE ABUSED BY TEACHERS OF THE PROSPERITY GOSPEL

I have heard something like this on many occasions: "Well, you have to be careful with verses like that because they're abused by the 'name it and claim it' crowd." If you are not familiar with what is variously called the prosperity gospel, Word of Faith movement, or the health-and-wealth gospel, it is a popular offshoot of the Pentecostal movement in America and now around the world. It is also popular on Christian television and radio worldwide and hence has an enormous footprint. One of the key teachings of this movement is that anyone with "faith" (not always well defined in a biblical sense) can, and should, be perfectly healthy and fabulously wealthy.

In their book *Health, Wealth, and Happiness*, David Jones

and Russell Woodbridge point out five basic theological errors made by teachers in this movement:

1. The Abrahamic covenant is a means to material entitlement.
2. Jesus's atonement extends to the "sin" of material poverty.
3. Christians give in order to gain material compensation from God.
4. Faith is a self-generated spiritual force that leads to prosperity.
5. Prayer is a tool to force God to grant prosperity.[1]

I will not comment on these points except to say they are at best not in the theological mainstream and at worst heretical. Either way, these teachings lay the foundation for some off-kilter Bible interpretation and application.

The verses in the New Testament that emphasize "asking and receiving" are, not surprisingly, favorites of the prosperity gospel teachers. Consider how one prosperity teacher, Robert Tilton, interprets John 15:7. According to Tilton, "Jesus was talking about *demanding your rights* and having restored back to you what the devil stole from man in the fall."[2] Prosperity teachers emphasize that there is a universal law by which even God is governed. Hence when we "ask," it can be a demand that God *has to obey*. This is a far cry from the loving and sovereign Father in heaven who delights to hear and respond to his children. The God of the prosperity gospel is more like a cosmic vending machine. You put in your money (the more money in, the more blessings out), demand your selection, and down will come the blessings of material goods and physical well-being.

One of the founding figures in the prosperity gospel movement, Kenneth Hagin, wrote this about John 15:7, "The Greek word translated 'ask' here means 'demand.' Demand whatsoever ye will and it shall be done unto you." By doing so, you call God's "attention to His part in the drama of life."[3]

It is easy to see how mainstream pastors, scholars, and Bible teachers would not want to be associated with this movement and hence why they would tend to shy away from passages that are used most often by prosperity gospel teachers. An unsavory arrogance, greed, and egocentric posture characterizes this approach to Christianity. And it simply isn't true and it is wildly misguided.

However, here is my response to this fear of guilt by association with verses that tend to be the favorites of the prosperity teachers such as John 15:7: *There is no way I am going to let those who abuse some of the most hopeful and upbeat sayings of Jesus keep me from getting every ounce of legitimate spiritual nourishment, gifting, and strength from them!*

Why should I forgo the tremendous blessings of fruit bearing that Jesus promised because some woefully imprudent ministers want to make it all about them and their lavish lifestyle? Not a chance. Rather than shy away from such passages because they are abused, I think we should recapture them for the Lord's true purpose and show our brothers and sisters a better way.

IT'S A CONDITIONAL PROMISE

This is a very important and legitimate point of qualification. As we've already noticed, John 15:7 is a "conditional promise." A conditional promise is a very simple concept. If you do x, then y will happen. You have to fulfill the "if" in order to realize the "then."

And in the case of John 15:7, there are two conditions, two "ifs" to be fulfilled before you see the "then" come to pass.

> *If* you remain (abide) in me and
>
> *if* my words remain (abide) in you,
>
> *[then]* ask whatever you wish,
>   and it will be done for you.

In light of this "if-then" construction, it makes perfect sense that if I am a Bible teacher who, for whatever reason, is uncomfortable with this kind of promise, that this would be the best place to justify why we are not getting what we pray for. And that is: We aren't fulfilling the conditions necessary to be given the things we request. We aren't living up to our part of the bargain. In some way or another, we are not abiding in him sufficiently, or his words are not abiding in us sufficiently. Therefore, we are not receiving what we ask for.

So that is the key question here, isn't it? Are we doing enough abiding to trigger the good result? It is a legitimate question—much more legitimate than some of the other objections I have heard. The answer, I think, for vast numbers of Christians is a resounding *yes*. *Yes,* we are sufficiently abiding to fulfill the conditional.

Let's take a quick look at what "abiding" is. The Greek word *meno* is most often translated into English as "remain" or "abide." I prefer "abide" because it captures the idea of an ongoing personal action better than "remain," which has a more passive connotation to it.

One of the best descriptions that I have heard that captures the notion of abiding in Christ is "to be at home with him." You love him, you trust him, and you invite him in as you would a faithful friend who always has your best interests in mind. You learn from him and know that following his advice or directions will always lead you down the right path, even if they are difficult words to hear sometimes. Abiding is the branch being plugged in tightly to the vine so the nourishment needed to bear fruit flows abundantly.

The second mention of "abide"—"if my words abide in you"—is not much different. But it focuses more directly on the specific teachings of Jesus rather than a family connection. Have you heard his advice and direction? Are you following through on them as Jesus the vine empowers you to do so?

Notice that abiding is accessible to every believer. Some commentators either over spiritualize this or focus too much on our efforts to accomplish this. Some seem to put abiding in Jesus in a category that only the spiritual elite might attain—that abiding in Jesus has to be done with a level of perfection that is a bit daunting or out of the reach of most.

But I think the text focuses on abiding as more of an attitude and a posture. Do you know that apart from him you can do nothing? Are you leaning into him for your daily spiritual growth and direction?

I am convinced this is available for all of us who follow Christ. One of the key reasons I think this is that Jesus was speaking these words to eleven men who were about to abandon him and deny him at a crucial hour. The temple guard was about to descend upon them in the Garden of Gethsemane, arrest Jesus, and begin the march toward his unjust execution. Even monumental failure on the part of the disciples was not going to eliminate them from abiding in Jesus and having his words abide in them in powerful ways. And neither will occasional sin and imperfection that lurches into our lives have power to separate us from the vine. There is nothing in the text about abiding *perfectly*. That is not a requirement.

In case you think you don't qualify for this promise, let me offer you one piece of evidence to the contrary: You are reading this book! Picking up a book devoted to abiding in Jesus, bearing his fruit, and being more effective in prayer sure suggests to me that you are likely abiding in him. In addition, I'll bet you attend church and care for the people God puts in your path in church, at home, or at work. I'm guessing you not only feed on the words of Jesus during the sermon on Sunday, but also during a midweek study or service. You might even listen to Bible teachers during your commute to work. Or perhaps you listen to worship music outside of church to be surrounded by thoughts of him. You read Scripture and pray regularly. How could this *not* be considered abiding in him and having his words abide in you?

Okay, you are not as consistent as you'd like. You really need to work on your fasting and being more generous to the needy. You feel inadequate before God so often, or even forget about him for days at a time. Well, join the club. But you keep coming back for more of him, don't you? Whether you feel that you are making progress or not, drawing closer to God and knowing his Word are always on the top of your list. With these feelings of inadequacy and the spiritual setbacks that we share even with the apostles, I still maintain, how could this *not* be considered abiding in him and having his words abide in you?

I am not going to try to quantify how many people abide in Jesus and how many don't—and I have no doubt that plenty of Christians are not abiding in the Lord. But I teach at a large Christian university. I travel constantly to teach, meet, and connect with Christians at a variety of churches. Based on the definition of "abiding" that I think is faithful to the text in John, I would say that the majority of the people I meet are abiding in the Lord and have his words abiding in them. This means there is really no good reason to turn this conditional statement into an escape hatch that can be used to explain why my prayers are not answered. If the conditions are met, the promise will be fulfilled.

So be of good cheer. I think you have good reason to

believe that you fulfill the first part of the conditional! Given what follows—"ask whatever you wish, and it will be done for you"—I think you have every reason to be very excited.

There is one more obstacle blocking our way to this ask-and-receive promise of Jesus. It is the mother of all barriers and one of the most powerful tools of the devil in the modern world—and it's especially good at undermining this amazing promise of Jesus.

CHAPTER 9

The Mother of All Barriers: Naturalism

One of the top movies in 1998 was a fun film called *The Truman Show*. The plot was outlandish but not so much so that it couldn't draw you in. It was the ultimate reality show. Actor Jim Carrey played Truman Burbank, who was supposed to be the star of the most popular live television show in history. The only problem is he doesn't know it. In fact, he lives in an island town and everything is a fabrication. All the buildings are part of an elaborate set, and all the inhabitants are scripted actors, including his wife. Almost every aspect of his day-to-day life in the town of Seahaven has been televised live since before his birth. Truman has never known anything different. His humdrum life as a desk clerk in an insurance office, his ordinary friends and neighbors, his ordinary wife, and his ordinary life have been monitored by the world through hidden cameras for 10,909 straight days.

But then things begin to change. Truman starts to pick up clues and mistakes by the production staff. Things just don't add up anymore. Those clues, combined with Truman's longing for travel and a different life, causes the whole thing to begin to unravel. And one day he discovers the truth and finds a way out. He waves farewell to his television audience and walks off the sound stage and out into the real world.

Truman Burbank had a view of the world that he picked up from his fabricated environment. He went on for almost thirty years with little reason to suspect things might be different.

We too walk around with views about the way the world really is that we pick up from our culture, family, friends, media, education, and so on. And for the most part, we have little reason to question our overall view of the world that is reinforced over and over again by all that surrounds us.

NATURALISM

Over the past three hundred years, a particular view of the world has come to dominate the way we see everything in the Western world. Philosophers and historians who study the history of ideas call this worldview *naturalism*.

Perhaps the easiest definition of naturalism is that nothing can be deemed legitimately supernatural. According to *The Stanford Encyclopedia of Philosophy*, naturalism basically means that "reality has no place for 'supernatural' or other 'spooky' kinds of entities." That is, the only things that exist are physical or material. That's why certain types of naturalism are often referred to as "physicalism" or "materialism." These are the kinds of things that can be studied by the hard sciences.

The famous astronomer and host of the popular *Cosmos* television series, Dr. Carl Sagan, had a saying that really captured the mindset of naturalism: "The Cosmos is all that is or ever was or ever will be." There is nothing apart from the physical stuff of the universe. This also means that pretty much everything in the universe has to be able to be explained by the laws of chemistry and physics. Matter, energy, space, and time exclusively and ultimately define all of reality, and the physical sciences are the only reliable ways to know that reality.

If you think about this depiction of naturalism even for a minute, it is clear that this is not a worldview that is going to be friendly toward Christianity or the spiritual life. After all, the Scriptures tell us that the most important entities in heaven and earth are not physical. God himself is spirit. We have souls that are nonphysical. There are angels and demons. We have moral principles. We are to pursue love, peace, joy, faith, humility, and justice—none of which are physical entities. We believe in a God who can heal, bring back people from the dead, cast out demons, change water into wine, and walk on water. None of this is allowed in the playbook of the physical sciences.

CHRISTIANITY VS. NATURALISM

By any measure Christianity provides a view of the world that is a dreadfully bad fit with naturalism. Naturalists look at the universe in dramatically different ways and have some vastly different values. Yet naturalism is by far the dominant worldview in our Western world today. And as the dominant view, there is no complete escape from it. Even Christian philosophers who are savvy in identifying and maneuvering around such worldly ideas find themselves affected by some aspects of them. We can't help it. We are all immersed in it. We all soak it up daily like a bitter marinade. We are like Truman Burbank wandering around in his hometown, soaking up the environment and not having a clue how vastly different things would look if we were to punch through the studio wall.

Most importantly for our study of Jesus's promise in John 15:7, naturalism has deeply affected those of us in the churches of the Western world. (The influence of naturalism has not been as dominant outside of North America and Europe, but I will not explore reasons for that here.) And the effects on us have been slow, subtle, steady, and profound. One of my very bright colleagues at Biola University, Dr. R. Scott Smith, has studied this and is alarmed by it:

> In fact, [naturalism] is subtle because most of us don't even recognize its pervasive influences on us as evangelicals, yet, if left untreated, it will utterly destroy us. *The problem is this: The evangelical churches in the west have been so deeply influenced (even unwittingly and unconsciously) by "naturalism" that we have been de-supernaturalized.* By and large, we have lost the power and presence of the Lord that is promised in Scripture, so that, to a dangerous degree, we are living in our own strength.[1]

These are sobering words. The people of God are supposed to be fundamentally supernatural people—those who fully expect a nonmaterial God to interact with their non-material souls. Smith's conclusion is that, in the modern age, the people of God have been "de-supernaturalized." That is, even Christians tend *not* to look beyond the confines of science for answers even to the biggest questions humans face. We tend to go along with naturalism without giving it a second thought.

For example, do you believe that your brain thinks? Do you believe that beauty is only in the eye of the beholder? When the New Testament speaks of eternal life, do you think it is not meant to be literal? Do you think memories are in your head? Do you think that you can know that lying is wrong for everyone just as surely as you can know that water freezes at 0° Celsius? Do you think that psychiatric medicine has properly replaced the ancient practice of exorcism in our culture? Do you think dreams are physical events in your brain? Do you believe human beings are fundamentally not different from other animals?

If you answered yes to any of these, you have probably been affected to some degree by naturalism. And you would be amazed at how many devoted Christians would answer yes to some or most of these. It would be fun to go through these questions right now to show you how they flow from the naturalist worldview and how they are opposed by the Christian worldview. I'll have to leave that for another time.

But I'll quickly address the first question as an example. Does your brain think? The answer is a resolute no, your brain does not think. Our minds, which are not material objects, do the thinking, not the brain. The brain is associated with our thinking, but it does not produce, change, or evaluate thoughts. Indeed, thoughts (the result of thinking) are not physical things, are they? No, they are not physical and cannot be measured or tested using the typical methods of scientific investigation. Thoughts do not have mass, charge, volume, shape, or color as physical objects have. But thoughts are as *real* as the book you are holding right now; they simply are not physical.

And this is what the Christian worldview holds: There are invisible entities that are not physical and that are not accessible to scientific investigation, but that are *real* and can be known to be as real as anything in the natural, physical world. There is much more to be said on this, but I will let it go here. The main points so far are that naturalism and Christianity set forth very different views of the world in which we live. And most Christians are deeply affected by and embrace a good deal of the naturalistic worldview.

JOHN 15:7 AND NATURALISM

The reason that naturalism is the "mother of all barriers" to us seeing Jesus's prayer promise fulfilled is obvious, is it not? After all, if we do not have a deep and steadfast belief that God exists and is in the business of at least occasionally intervening in our lives in supernatural ways, we are not likely to believe that God will respond to prayer requests, right?

But perhaps someone might say, "Hey, look, I'm not an atheist. I do believe in God and that he can answer prayer, so this doesn't apply to me." That person does not recognize that their belief that God will respond to a prayer in a super-natural way is diminished at some level because of their life-long contact with our naturalistic environment. This is what I recognized years ago sitting in my "comfy Bible-reading chair" that I mentioned in the first chapter. I suddenly awoke to the idea that Jesus really meant what he said, and something was keeping me from taking it seriously.

I believe the main barrier to my embracing this fully was the naturalistic mindset—it had enveloped me more thoroughly than I recognized. I believed in God. I believed he could and would answer prayer. But I did not fully buy into the idea that he would answer prayer in the definitive way Jesus described in verses such as John 15:7; 14:13-14;

Matthew 7:7-8; 18:19; 21:21-22; Mark 11:24, and so on. And I am not alone in this. At some level our culture's commitment to naturalism affects all of us. And I believe it is the main reason that even faithful Bible believers have trouble embracing Jesus's promise exactly in the bold way Jesus states it.

Several years ago one of my former students who was from Africa came to my office to visit me. His name was Kojo. He had completed a master's degree in my graduate program in Christian apologetics and was then doing ministry in his home country of Ghana. He had traveled to the states and was kind enough to stop by.

As we talked, Kojo described some amazing miracles of God that he had witnessed during his times of ministry. On a somewhat regular basis people were healed, demons were cast out, and dramatic prayers were answered. He even described a mother carrying a dead son into one of their meetings. After prayer the boy came back to life. I was amazed. I could have listened to his accounts of God's supernatural work all day. But at one point I stopped him and asked an obvious question.

"Kojo, why do you think we don't see this level of supernatural activity here in America?"

Kojo looked at me strangely for a moment. Then he

smiled and said, "I can't believe you have to ask that. Isn't the answer obvious to you?"

It was pretty clear by the look on my face that I didn't have a clue what the obvious answer was.

"I can't believe you don't know," he said again, enjoying the fact that he was keeping me in suspense.

So I grabbed his arm and said, "Tell me!"

He laughed and said, "The reason you don't see as much supernatural activity in your country is because you have 911."

I looked puzzled again.

"You know, 911—the emergency phone number," he said. "You can have medics anywhere you are in minutes. If someone is hurt or there's danger or a tragic accident, you call 911. It's the first thing you do. And help is on the way immediately.

"Where I minister in Ghana we don't have 911. We don't have expert help minutes away. So you know what we do first? We pray. And so we pray a lot—a lot more than you do here because God is our first and often our only hope. And God often shows up in a powerful way. He doesn't heal everyone we pray for, not everyone is saved from harm, not every need is met. But we pray. And because we pray often and we put our trust in God, we see amazing things happen on a fairly regular basis. We ask God to help us. It is our first response. And you know what? I have no doubt that we see God's hand move much more often than you do here in America simply because we pray more often. We don't have an alternative. Of course, after you see God answer your prayer for help several times in difficult circumstances, it becomes a habit. We pray, we believe, and we see God move."

Kojo did not grow up in an environment awash in naturalism, but we did. And this story illustrates the differences that result. He was immediately ready to pray and was wide open to the supernatural intervention of God. His view of the world was filled with the supernatural and he was accustomed to go there *first*. Those of us who dial 911 first are less conditioned to respond with immediate prayers and cries to God. We tend to trust first in our well-trained first responders, advanced communications ability, and medical science.

Now please don't think that I am saying we should not dial 911. Heaven forbid. Such a service is a wonderful gift of common grace from God and can be used by God to save lives and avert tragedy. While it is good to use these services, we are not to put our ultimate trust in them. We are to reserve that ultimate trust for God. The naturalism we are immersed in everyday, though, fights against us.

Every age seems to have some dominant idea or collection

of ideas designed to divert faithful believers from their greatest source of power in God. In our age, few things can rival naturalism in its ability to remove our gaze from God's Word and refocus it on false and powerless thinking. It is really a form of spiritual warfare—spiritual warfare the apostle Paul was very familiar with. Although naturalism was not the troublesome idea of his day, Paul warned us of powerful obstacles from the world of ideas that will block our spiritual path. He encouraged every one of us to "demolish arguments and every pretention that sets itself up against the knowledge of God, and we take captive every thought to make it obedient to Christ" (2 Corinthians 10:5). As best we can, we are to be aware of and counter those worldviews that stand to rob us of our very best tools for ministry and communion with God.

Because we are immersed in naturalism, though, it is hard to recognize all its effects. So prayer about it is important. Here then is a prayer that God will hear and answer: "Help me to see through the fog of naturalistic thinking in which I am immersed. Help me demolish arguments and pretentions that block my pure knowledge of you and your kingdom purposes."

A steadfast recognition of God's supernatural power in our lives will do wonders in overcoming the curse of naturalism in our culture and in our prayer lives.

If we have been able to extract ourselves from our naturalistic thinking, there is only one more thing we need to address before we have full access to the Lord's outrageous promise in John 15:7.

CHAPTER 10

Revealing the Full Weight of the Promise

I always knew I would try to earn a PhD someday. I had research, teaching, and the world of ideas in my blood. As an undergraduate I started out as a biology major and thought I would go into medical research. That sounded like a good way to make a decent living. But along the way, I decided that philosophy, theology, and religious studies sounded even more delicious when it came to debating and classroom discussions. (Obviously I was not thinking clearly about the long-term financial ramifications of my subject of study.)

I had a definite kingdom vision in mind for my future too. I had been a Christian for about four years by then and I loved doing evangelism and apologetics—especially answering the questions and objections that college students had about all the big issues of life. I saw myself as a tenured professor of religious studies at a secular school—a difficult thing for a committed Christian to achieve. I had bumped into a rare Christian professor or two on my secular campus as an undergraduate and found them so encouraging and helpful. I wanted to do the same thing.

I prayed that God would show me the proper path to take to get to the goal. I applied to one of the top secular graduate programs in the field of religious studies—and praise God, I was accepted (miracle one). I was newly married and prayed for and applied for inexpensive student housing that had a two-year waiting list. It was a nail biter, but we were notified that we had been granted very affordable housing just days before classes started. And it was the best student housing on the campus (miracle two).

It was a hostile atmosphere for a Jesus-loving, Bible-reading guy like me. At one of the first faculty-student gatherings I attended, one of the top professors in the department said, "I think we can all agree that one of the greatest evils we face today is the global presence of conservative religious believers." (Of course, he meant guys like me—welcome to the department!) But despite this built-in suspicion and antagonism, the Lord gave me tremendous favor in my work in the department and with my relationships with the professors and other graduate students (miracle three).

We were able to pay for my grad school because my wife was working as a nurse, and I was able to work as a teaching and research assistant. We were able to eke out a financial existence without loans, which we were thrilled about. When I progressed to researching and writing my doctoral dissertation, I had to cut back on work. But my wife was pregnant with our first child, so she couldn't work as much. We were starting to feel a serious financial pinch. We prayed that the Lord would sustain us.

I took a month or two to identify every scholarship I could even remotely qualify for and applied for every one of them. I received *all* of them! It was crazy. Every day I'd get another check in the mail—and they were big ones. It wasn't just that my wife and I made it through without going into debt. It was that we made it through the last couple of years without any financial worries whatsoever. We even had enough after grad school to put toward a down payment on a house. That's just not what happens in graduate school.

The chair of the department told me that in all his years at the university, he had never seen a grad student win so many scholarship awards. He was certain that I held a record that would not soon be broken (over-the-top miracle four).

THE CRUCIAL CONTEXT: FRUIT BEARING

This time in graduate school was one of the most prayer-responsive times of my life. I still look back on it with awe. There is no doubt that this story puts on display amazing blessings toward me from God. I felt his warmth, care, and favor in very tangible ways.

After years of reflection on this experience, and many others like it since, I'd have to say there was something special about the nature of the prayer requests I delivered to God that played an important role in receiving these blessings. It was not about clever wording, persuasive phrases, eloquence, or the length of my prayer oration. And it certainly wasn't because I had some better-than-average standing with God, or something like that. No, it was simply that all the prayers during my challenging experience in graduate school were, by nature, about *fruit bearing*. I was going to school for the sole purpose of receiving high-level training for unique ministry purposes.

Bearing fruit for the Lord is the overall context of this passage we have been studying in the Gospel of John. As we have already seen, from John 15:1 to 15:17 it is all about the vine, the branches, and bearing abundant fruit. So when we read the great prayer promise in John 15:7 about asking and receiving, it comes right in the middle of this discourse focusing on fruit bearing and is intimately linked with it.

Well, if fruit bearing is so important, then what is it exactly? We haven't done anything more than mention it thus far. So, what is this fruit? To what is this central spiritual metaphor referring?

Modern scholars agree that the fruit borne by Jesus's followers, and later by us today, can be vast and diverse.[1] One simple and comprehensive definition is this: being about the Father's business in an effectual way. Or, any kind of personal growth or activity that leads to a positive expression or expansion of the kingdom of God. Or, using a football analogy, bearing fruit is moving the ball down the field toward the kingdom goal line. It really is that simple, and we ought not to overthink it.

At the same time, it is profound in its implications. For clarity, I have broken fruit bearing down into the following three basic categories with examples.

Obvious ministry and church related service. This kind of fruit bearing includes things like working in the nursery at church, taking a late-night phone call from a troubled member of the youth group, working on the church parking team, doing the registration work for Vacation Bible School, driving the bus to the church retreat, writing a new worship song, learning Japanese so you can be an effective witness on your mission trip, preparing a Bible study lesson, serving on the board of elders, serving communion, giving generously during the offering, and so on. Notice they can be high-profile to very low-profile activities. All that are done with a heart to assist with kingdom work count.

Personal Christian growth. These are activities or efforts that lead to advances and maturity in the Lord, such as deeper Bible reading, mentoring by mature believers, and spiritual disciplines such as solitude and fasting. These are all designed to lead to a greater development and deployment of the fruits of the Spirit in our lives: love, joy, peace, patience, goodness, kindness, gentleness, faithfulness, and self-control, and all the good deeds and benefits to the community that result from serious character development in the Lord.

Everyday work in Jesus's name. These are all the things we do every day in Jesus's name outside of typical church or ministry boundaries. Put another way, these are the things we do for Jesus's sake and with kingdom progress specifically in mind, such as working extra hours at your secular job so you can have money to sponsor a kid on the high school retreat, sharing the gospel with another parent at a Little League game, volunteering at the local crisis pregnancy center, opening your home to flood victims, being a mentor to the boy down the street who lost his dad, or enrolling in a challenging graduate program so that you will have the training necessary to proclaim and defend the faith in arenas other Christians can't.

You can see that fruit-bearing activities are about as vast as our kingdom imaginations can take us. In his commentary on the Gospel of John, New Testament scholar D.A. Carson warns us against envisioning "fruit" in a way that is too narrow. He sees it as an immense range of kingdom activities and that this "fruit is nothing less than the outcome of persevering dependence on the vine, driven by faith, embracing all of the believer's life and the product of his witness."[2] And it is these kinds of kingdom activities, hopes, and dreams to which the prayer model in John 15:7 applies so seamlessly.

THE PROMISE FULLY
REVEALED AND REALIZED

So we have come to the end of the historical analysis, the exposition, the interpretation, the conditional. We have answered the objections and qualifications, we have avoided the prayer poison in our culture that is naturalism, and we have a keen understanding of the overall context of fruit bearing.

We are now at a place to see how the radical promise of John 15:7 actually plays out. Here it is:

☑ If you remain in me
☑ And my words remain in you
☑ And you are focused on bearing fruit for the Lord

then

ask whatever you wish, and it will be done for you.

You can ask with great certainty because:

The Lord himself has promised this (John 15:7).

He does not lie (Hebrews 6:18).

He is absolutely faithful in doing what he promises (Isaiah 55:11).

CHAPTER 11

This Is to My Father's Glory

Theologians have trouble finding words to describe John 15:7 and similar passages, such as John 14:12-14 and Matthew 7:7-8. Klaus Issler, who has written thoughtfully on these provocative sections of Scripture, says, "In response to this promise, evangelical commentators use words such as *staggering, breathtaking, startling, astonishing*.[1] J.I. Packer says, "In his farewell discourse to the apostles Jesus spoke more than once of making requests to the Father in his name—with astounding promises attached," and, "Amazing! But that is what Jesus says, and all his words are true."[2] The famous prayer servant George Müller put it this way: "Our difficulty seems to be this: the promise is so 'exceeding great' that we cannot conceive God really to mean what he clearly appears to have revealed. The blessing seems too vast for our comprehension; we 'stagger at the promises.'"[3]

The very next verse, John 15:8, is a wonderfully affirming statement from Jesus about the abiding and asking he just encouraged us to do. He said, "This is to my Father's glory, that you bear much fruit, showing yourselves to be my disciples." It's as if the Father is standing outside our prayer room right now with a basket filled with every good thing we might need—spiritual gifts, personal insight, funding, ready helpers, ministry tools—to be productive in his kingdom work. As New Testament scholar Frank Scott said over a century ago, "What a blessed promise this is to those who can fully appropriate it!"[4]

TWO TYPES OF ASKING

I think it's clear by now that there is a special type of asking going on in John 15:7 that accesses the promise—and that is, asking with focused kingdom issues in mind. But we find ourselves asking God regularly for things that may not be mission critical for spiritual fruit bearing, hence they seem outside of what Jesus had in mind here. Are those requests legitimate? Yes, of course they are. We have many needs and wants that are not on the front lines of fruit bearing, and God is attentive to those. Let me see if I can explain with an analogy.

When my four kids were young, they would ask me to buy them things—an American Girl doll, a special video game, an ice-cream cone, and the like. Like any engaged parent, I would evaluate on a case-by-case basis using a whole range of factors: What does it cost? Is it good for them? Will it distract from school? Is it too close to dinnertime? So in the course of relationship with me, they would ask but they would not always receive the things they were asking for. They couldn't absolutely count on getting what they asked for, and they knew that.

However, it was a different story if they asked for something that clearly was going to help them with personal growth, health, school, or a future career. If they asked for an SAT study book, money for an inner-city mission trip, eyeglasses, a special study Bible, new running shoes, I would move mountains to try to get those things to them. I think the same thing is true with God. When we ask for things that will bring fruit bearing and kingdom advance into play, he is on it. According to John 15:7, we can take it to the bank—and God's resources for providing those things are limitless.

However, if we ask him for a new set of golf clubs or a weekend in Aspen (assuming there are no discernible fruit-bearing aspects to the request), it is not as certain. God will work with us too about these requests, and we can trust him to evaluate them properly. He has the power to do so, and we can count on his love. So we should ask—even if it is not a mission-critical request. Here's why.

First, God enjoys blessing us with good gifts in the same way I enjoy giving special gifts to my children. Second, it is all part of building a valuable communication relationship with the Father. As we lay our wants, dreams, and goals before him, he searches us and speaks back to us. As J.I. Packer noticed, when we have a prayer conversation with God, "He is asking questions about our asking."[5] He searches our hearts and gently interacts with our request. Why do you ask for this? How serious is the matter? How do you think this aligns with my will? And so on. Requests of any kind open the door to communication with the Father for a serious believer. Even if, as James warns (James 4:3), we ask with "wrong motives," it ushers us into a time with God and provides opportunities for correction and for direct discipleship from the Holy Spirit. As Simon Chan said, "Real asking, giving, and receiving are deep interchanges between friends."[6]

So ask him!

ASKING IS THE RULE OF THE KINGDOM

In a sermon in London in 1882, the famous British preacher Charles H. Spurgeon delivered a sermon titled "Ask and Have." In this message he said,

> Do you know, brothers and sisters, *what great things are to be had for the asking?* Have you ever thought of it? Does it not stimulate you to pray fervently? All heaven lies before the grasp of the asking man, all the promises of God are rich and inexhaustible, and their fulfillment is to be had by prayer…Thus you see the Lord's promises have many fulfillments, and they are all waiting now to pour their treasures into the lap of prayer. Does not this lift prayer up to a high level, when God is willing to repeat the biographies of His saints in us, when He is waiting to be gracious, and to load us with His benefits? I will mention another truth which ought to make us pray, and that is, that *if we ask, God will give to us much more than we ask.*

After a long discourse on the mind-boggling power and benefits God has put at our disposal through prayer, Spurgeon concludes, "*Asking is the rule of the kingdom.*"[7]

Of course, this focus on asking did not start with Spurgeon. We have already seen that it is the decided posture of Scripture, and it carried through strongly to the earliest church. Indeed, one of the earliest writings of the Apostolic Fathers, the Shepherd of Hermas, from around AD 170, says it for the ages.

> How can I ask for something from God and receive it, when I have sinned so often against him? Do not reason in this way, but turn to the Lord with all your heart and ask of him unhesitatingly, and you will know his extraordinary compassion, because he will never abandon you but will fulfill your soul's request…Ask of the Lord and you will receive everything, and [you] will not fail to receive all of your requests…So cleanse your heart of double-mindedness and put on faith, because it is strong, and trust God that you will receive all the requests you make.[8]

COME AND SEE WHAT OUR FATHER WILL DO

George Müller is a legend in the realm of prayer and trusting God. If you have never heard of him, I'm delighted to introduce you to him. If you do know him already, I'm happy to remind you about him. I would be negligent not including at least a word about him in a book like this.

Müller started several homes for orphans in Bristol, England. His first was opened in 1836 for thirty children, and by 1870 he was caring for over two thousand children. He was a man of prayer who documented in diaries around fifty thousand prayers, thirty thousand of which were answered within twenty-four hours of the request being made. Müller is known to have run a range of orphanages and other ministries without ever asking anybody for money.

One of his legendary answers to prayer took place around 1861 in Bristol and is recorded firsthand by his colleague's daughter Abigail Townsend. Abigail was playing in a garden near the orphanage when Müller came out, took her by the hand, and said, "Come and see what our Father will do."

Abigail recounts entering a long dining room with empty plates, cups, and bowls lining the table. All the children of the orphanage were standing around the table waiting for breakfast. What Abigail did not know at the time was that there was not a morsel of food in the house.

"Children, you know that we must be in time for school," said Müller. And lifting his hand he prayed, "Dear Father, we thank Thee for what Thou art going to give us to eat."

Not moments later there was a knock at the door. It was a baker who said to Müller, "I couldn't sleep last night. Somehow I felt you didn't have bread for breakfast, and the Lord wanted me to send you some. So I got up at two o'clock and baked some fresh bread, and have brought it."

A second knock was heard soon thereafter. This time it was the milkman. "Müller, my milk cart has broken down outside the orphanage. I would like to give the children the cans of fresh milk so that they can empty the wagon and repair it." They thanked the baker and the milkman and they all enjoyed their breakfast.[9] In Müller's mind, there was simply no way that God would not do this.

OPPORTUNITIES ON YOUR DOORSTEP

You can't read the exploits of George Müller and not be inspired to jump in and do something great through God in your own life. And of course, Müller could not read passages like John 15:7 and not be inspired to live on the edge and watch God gloriously do what he promised.

The Father has certainly laid some tremendous fruit-bearing opportunities at your doorstep, and he would be thrilled to have you jump into the kingdom labor pool. It will be his great pleasure to meet you there with all the tools, gifts, and needs according to your prayers to accomplish some tasks with eternal weight.

Understanding as best I can what Jesus said in John 15:7

has transformed my prayer life and kingdom work. If I am abiding in him, and his words are abiding in me, and I have some kind of ministry or fruit-bearing need, I pray for it and expect to receive it. There really is no other way to understand John 15:7. And if I do not receive it right away, I keep praying. How can he not answer? As Spurgeon wrote, "The promise is the power of prayer. We go to God and we say to him, 'Do as thou hast said, O Lord, here is thy word; we beseech thee fulfill it.'"

Postscript

Jesus's words on prayer in the Gospels were meant to inspire us to be deeply dependent on the Father for everything and to dream big about our kingdom impact. In this book I have given special attention to petitionary prayer focused on bearing fruit for the Lord—and I hope it encouraged you in a profound way. But regrettably there is so much more that I did not cover.

For instance, I did not address the very important prayers for physical healing or prayers for individual salvation. There is no doubt we should pray fervently for such things. To be sure, if we pray more diligently than we do now, we will see God's hand move in these areas more frequently and in powerful ways.

However, there are special issues and nuances about praying for healing and for salvation that go beyond the scope of this book. If you would like to know more about those special features, you can find some of my thoughts and some resources I recommend at my book website **www.fearlessprayer.com**.

And once you start to put this into practice, I'd be delighted for you to tell us all how the Lord is answering your prayers. You can post your encouraging experiences to that same website.

Helpful Bible Passages About Prayer

The Word of God provides tremendous motivation to fix our attention on God and his kingdom purposes through prayer. Below is a selection of brief Scripture passages worthy of regular meditation.

These verses remind us that we can be fearless and confident to bring our lives and prayers before Almighty God. They remind us through direction and example the benefits of being devoted to prayer. And they remind us that God sees asking, receiving, and fruit-bearing as a vital part of our ongoing relationship with him and his kingdom.

BRING YOUR PRAYERS
CONFIDENTLY BEFORE GOD

Ephesians 3:12

In him and through faith in him we may approach God with freedom and confidence.

Hebrews 4:16

Let us then approach God's throne of grace with confidence, so that we may receive mercy and find grace to help us in our time of need.

Hebrews 10:19-22

Since we have confidence to enter the Most Holy Place by the blood of Jesus, by a new and living way opened for us through the curtain, that is, his body, and since we have a great priest over the house of God, let us draw near to God with a sincere heart and with the full assurance that faith brings.

1 John 3:21-22

Dear friends, if our hearts do not condemn us, we have confidence before God and receive from him anything we ask, because we keep his commands and do what pleases him.

1 John 5:14-15

This is the confidence we have in approaching God: that if we ask anything according to his will, he hears us. And if we know that he hears us—whatever we ask—we know that we have what we asked of him.

Romans 8:26

In the same way, the Spirit helps us in our weakness. We do not know what we ought to pray for, but the Spirit himself intercedes for us through wordless groans.

BEING DEEPLY DEVOTED TO GOD THROUGH PRAYER

Psalm 5:2

Hear my cry for help,
my King and my God,
for to you I pray.
In the morning, LORD, you hear my voice;
in the morning I lay my requests before you
and wait expectantly.

Daniel 6:10

Now when Daniel learned that the decree had been

published, he went home to his upstairs room where the windows opened toward Jerusalem. Three times a day he got down on his knees and prayed, giving thanks to his God, just as he had done before.

Matthew 14:23

After he had dismissed them, he went up on a mountainside by himself to pray.

Mark 1:35-37

Very early in the morning, while it was still dark, Jesus got up, left the house and went off to a solitary place, where he prayed. Simon and his companions went to look for him, and when they found him, they exclaimed: "Everyone is looking for you!"

Luke 5:15-16

Yet the news about him spread all the more, so that crowds of people came to hear him and to be healed of their sicknesses. But Jesus often withdrew to lonely places and prayed.

Acts 1:14

They all joined together constantly in prayer, along with the women and Mary the mother of Jesus, and with his brothers.

Romans 12:12

Be joyful in hope, patient in affliction, faithful in prayer.

Philippians 4:6-7

Do not be anxious about anything, but in every situation, by prayer and petition, with thanksgiving, present your requests to God. And the peace of God, which transcends all understanding, will guard your hearts and your minds in Christ Jesus.

Colossians 4:2

Devote yourselves to prayer, being watchful and thankful.

1 Thessalonians 5:16-18

Rejoice always, pray continually, give thanks in all circumstances; for this is God's will for you in Christ Jesus.

1 Timothy 2:8

Therefore I want the men everywhere to pray, lifting up holy hands without anger or disputing.

ASKING IS CENTRAL TO OUR
COMMUNICATION WITH GOD

1 Chronicles 4:10

Jabez cried out to the God of Israel, "Oh, that you would bless me and enlarge my territory! Let your hand be with me, and keep me from harm so that I will be free from pain." And God granted his request.

2 Chronicles 1:7-12

That night God appeared to Solomon and said to him, "Ask for whatever you want me to give you."…Solomon answered God…"Give me wisdom and knowledge, that I may lead this people, for who is able to govern this great people of yours?"

God said to Solomon, "Since this is your heart's desire… therefore wisdom and knowledge will be given you. And I will also give you wealth, possessions and honor, such as no king who was before you ever had and none after you will have."

Psalm 20:5

May we shout for joy over your victory
    and lift up our banners in the name of our God.
May the LORD grant all your requests.

Isaiah 58:9

Then you will call, and the LORD will answer;
you will cry for help, and he will say: Here am I.

Isaiah 65:24

Before they call I will answer;
while they are still speaking I will hear.

Matthew 6:6

When you pray, go into your room, close the door and pray to your Father, who is unseen. Then your Father, who sees what is done in secret, will reward you.

Matthew 6:7-8

When you pray, do not keep on babbling like pagans, for they think they will be heard because of their many words. Do not be like them, for your Father knows what you need before you ask him.

Matthew 7:7-8

Ask and it will be given to you; seek and you will find; knock and the door will be opened to you. For everyone who asks receives; the one who seeks finds; and to the one who knocks, the door will be opened.

Matthew 7:11

> If you, then, though you are evil, know how to give good gifts to your children, how much more will your Father in heaven give good gifts to those who ask him!

Matthew 18:19-20

> Again, truly I tell you that if two of you on earth agree about anything they ask for, it will be done for them by my Father in heaven. For where two or three gather in my name, there am I with them.

Mark 11:22-24

> "Have faith in God," Jesus answered. "Truly I tell you, if anyone says to this mountain, 'Go, throw yourself into the sea,' and does not doubt in their heart but believes that what they say will happen, it will be done for them. Therefore I tell you, whatever you ask for in prayer, believe that you have received it, and it will be yours."

John 11:41-42

> Then Jesus looked up and said, "Father, I thank you that you have heard me. I knew that you always hear me, but I said this for the benefit of the people standing here, that they may believe that you sent me."

John 14:12-14

Very truly I tell you, whoever believes in me will do the works I have been doing, and they will do even greater things than these, because I am going to the Father. And I will do whatever you ask in my name, so that the Father may be glorified in the Son. You may ask me for anything in my name, and I will do it.

John 15:7

If you remain in me and my words remain in you, ask whatever you wish, and it will be done for you.

Philippians 4:19

My God will meet all your needs according to the riches of his glory in Christ Jesus.

Colossians 1:9-10

For this reason, since the day we heard about you, we have not stopped praying for you. We continually ask God to fill you with the knowledge of his will through all the wisdom and understanding that the Spirit gives, so that you may live a life worthy of the Lord and please him in every way: bearing fruit in every good work.

2 Thessalonians 1:11-12

With this in mind, we constantly pray for you, that our God may make you worthy of his calling, and that by his power he may bring to fruition your every desire for goodness and your every deed prompted by faith. We pray this so that the name of our Lord Jesus may be glorified in you, and you in him, according to the grace of our God and the Lord Jesus Christ.

James 1:5

If any of you lacks wisdom, you should ask God, who gives generously to all without finding fault, and it will be given to you.

James 5:16

The prayer of a righteous person is powerful and effective.

Notes

CHAPTER 2–DOES THIS STUFF REALLY HAPPEN?

1. James Taylor, "More Miraculous Moments" in James L. Garlow and Keith Wall, *Real Life, Real Miracles* (Minneapolis, MN: Bethany House Publishers, 2012), 227-29.

2. Rosalind Goforth, *How I Know God Answers Prayer* (Philadelphia: Sunday School Times Company, 1921), 16-17.

CHAPTER 3–PRAYER: STRANGE, POWERFUL, AND REAL

1. J.I. Packer and Carolyn Nystrom, *Praying: Finding Our Way Through Duty to Delight* (Downers Grove, IL: IVP Books, 2006), 9.

2. Packer and Nystrom, *Praying*, 149.

3. Dallas Willard, *The Divine Conspiracy: Rediscovering Our Hidden Life in God* (San Francisco: HarperSanFrancisco, 1998), 241-42.

4. Dallas Willard, *The Spirit of the Disciplines: Understanding How God Changes Lives* (New York: HarperOne, 1988), 184.

CHAPTER 4–REASONS TO BELIEVE

1. See Gary R. Habermas, *The Risen Jesus and Future Hope* (Lanham, MD: Rowman and Littlefield Publishers, 2003), 9-10.

CHAPTER 5–I AM THE VINE AND YOU ARE THE BRANCHES

1. Robert H. Mounce, "The Gospel of John," *The Expositor's Bible Commentary, Revised Edition*, Tremper Longman III and David E. Garland, gen. eds. (Grand Rapids, MI: Zondervan, 2007), 10:574.

2. Mounce, "The Gospel of John," 10:575.

CHAPTER 7—DEATH BY A THOUSAND QUALIFICATIONS

1. Richard J. Foster, *Prayer: Finding the Heart's True Home* (San Francisco: HarperSanFrancisco, 1992), 179.

CHAPTER 8—FROM ABUSING TO ABIDING

1. See David W. Jones and Russell S. Woodbridge, *Health, Wealth, and Happiness: Has the Prosperity Gospel Overshadowed the Gospel of Christ?* (Grand Rapids, MI: Kregel, 2011).

2. Robert Tilton, *To Catch a Thief* (Dallas, TX: Word of Faith, 1988), 88-89. Emphasis mine.

3. Kenneth E. Hagin, *Plead Your Case* (Tulsa, OK: Kenneth Hagin Ministries, 1979), 2.

CHAPTER 9—THE MOTHER OF ALL BARRIERS: NATURALISM

1. R. Scott Smith, "Our Great Evangelical Disaster: The De-Supernaturalization of the Evangelical Church in the West, and What to Do about It" (unpublished manuscript, 2016). Emphasis Smith's.

CHAPTER 10—REVEALING THE FULL WEIGHT OF THE PROMISE

1. See Andreas J. Köstenberger, *John* (Grand Rapids, MI: Baker Academic, 2004), 454.

2. D.A. Carson, *The Gospel According to John* (Grand Rapids, MI: William B. Eerdmans, 1991), 517.

CHAPTER 11—THIS IS TO MY FATHER'S GLORY

1. Klaus Issler, *Living into the Life of Jesus* (Downers Grove, IL: IVP Books, 2012), 151. Emphasis Issler's.

2. Packer and Nystrom, *Praying*, 153, 215.

3. George Müller, *The Life of Trust* (New York: Thomas Y. Crowell and Company, 1898), xviii.

4. W. Frank Scott, *A Homiletic Commentary on the Gospel of St. John*, reprint ed. (Grand Rapids, MI: Baker Books, 1996), 426.

5. Packer and Nystrom, *Praying*, 152.

6. Simon Chan, *Spiritual Theology: A Systematic Study of the Christian Life* (Downers Grove, IL: InterVarsity Press, 1998), 140.

7. Charles H. Spurgeon, "Ask and Have," a sermon delivered at the Metropolitan Tabernacle, London, on 1 October 1882, www.spurgeongems.org/vols28-30/chs1682 .pdf. Emphasis Spurgeon's.

8. "The Shepherd of Hermas" in *The Apostolic Fathers: Greek Texts and English Translations*, 3d ed., Michael W. Holmes, trans. ed. (Grand Rapids, MI: Baker Academic, 2007), 533.

9. Roger Steer, *George Müller: Delighted in God* (Ross-shire, Great Britain: Christian Focus Publications, 1997), 134.

ABOUT THE AUTHOR

D r. Craig Hazen is Professor of Comparative Religion and Christian Apologetics at Biola University and founder and director of the Christian Apologetics Program. He holds a PhD in religious studies from the University of California, a degree in biological sciences, and studied international law and human rights in Strasbourg, France.

He is the author or contributor to a range of books, including *To Everyone an Answer*, *The Apologetics Study Bible*, *The Case for Grace*, *Apologetics for a New Generation*, and his acclaimed novel, *Five Sacred Crossings*.

Dr. Hazen is a sought-after speaker and has engaged audiences all over North America, Europe, and Asia on effective prayer, the evidence for the resurrection, religion and science, and Christianity among world religions. He has also spoken multiple times on Capitol Hill and in the White House. At Biola, he was named the winner of the highest award for faculty excellence.

Dr. Hazen is a former cohost of a national talk radio program and a regular on-camera expert for broadcast television. He and his wife, Karen, live in Southern California and have four grown children.

If you would like Dr. Hazen to speak at your event, church, or school, or you would like to know more about his books, blogs, and videos, you can contact him through his website at

www.craighazen.com

To learn more about Harvest House books and
to read sample chapters, visit our website:

www.harvesthousepublishers.com

HARVEST HOUSE PUBLISHERS
EUGENE, OREGON